# Garfield
## FAT CAT 3-PACK
### VOLUME 14

# Garfield
# FAT CAT 3-PACK
## VOLUME 14

BY
JIM DAVIS

BALLANTINE BOOKS • NEW YORK

2009 Ballantine Books Trade Paperback Edition



Based on the Garfield® characters created by Jim Davis.

Published in the United States by Ballantine Books, an imprint of Random House, a division of Penguin Random House LLC.

GARFIELD SURVIVAL OF THE FATTEST, GARFIELD OLDER & WIDER, and GARFIELD PIGS OUT were each published separately by Ballantine Books, an imprint of Random House, a division of Penguin Random House LLC, New York, in 2004, 2005, and 2006 respectively.



ISBN 978-0-345-49175-6

Printed in China

randomhousebooks.com

14 13

# Garfield
## SURVIVAL of the FATTEST

BY JIM DAVIS

Ballantine Books • New York

# Outrageous Outtakes

**Never-before-seen, over-the-top strips saved from extinctio by our kooky comics conservationist.**

GARFIELD®
ALMOST READY...
Distributed by Universal Press Syndicate
KACHING!
CLONK
MY EYE!
HOT! HOT! HOT! HOT! HOT! HOT!
SPLORT!
WAAAAH
SCHLIIIP!
© 2001 PAWS, INC. All Rights Reserved.
HERE'S YOUR TOAST
I THINK I'LL JUST HAVE A COLD BAGEL INSTEAD
JIM DAVIS 6·3

WAKE UP, GARFIELD!
THE WHOLE WORLD IS WAITING FOR YOU!
TELL THE WORLD TO GET A LIFE
JIM DAVIS 6-4
Distributed by Universal Press Syndicate www.garfield.com
© 2001 PAWS, INC. All Rights Reserved.

I REALLY SHOULD CUT THE GRASS... BUT IT'S SUCH A NICE DAY
MAYBE I'LL WATER IT INSTEAD
WHAT'S WITH THE SUNGLASSES?
YOU'RE BLINDING ME WITH YOUR LOGIC
JIM DAVIS 6-5
Distributed by Universal Press Syndicate www.garfield.com
© 2001 PAWS, INC. All Rights Reserved.

I THOUGHT ODIE WAS CHASING YOU AROUND THE TREE OUT BACK
HE IS
I DON'T THINK HE'S CAUGHT ME YET
JIM DAVIS 6-6
Distributed by Universal Press Syndicate www.garfield.com
© 2001 PAWS, INC. All Rights Reserved.

THERE WERE THREE DOZEN COOKIES ON THIS PLATE...
AND NOW THEY'RE GONE!
BAD PLATE!
JIM DAVIS 6-7
Distributed by Universal Press Syndicate www.garfield.com
© 2001 PAWS, INC. All Rights Reserved.

YOU KNOW, ODIE...
THE SECRET TO LOOKING GOOD IS TO ACCESSORIZE
JIM DAVIS 6-8
Distributed by Universal Press Syndicate www.garfield.com
© 2001 PAWS, INC. All Rights Reserved.

YOU KNOW, GARFIELD, I'M NOT REALLY BORING
I'M MELLOW
I HAVE A LAID-BACK PERSONALITY
THAT'S WHY WE BURIED IT IN THE BACKYARD THREE YEARS AGO
JIM DAVIS 6-9
Distributed by Universal Press Syndicate www.garfield.com
© 2001 PAWS, INC. All Rights Reserved.

GARFIELD
AH, THE SIMPLE, DIRECT APPROACH
BEWARE OF DOG
www.garfield.com
SELF-EXPLANATORY
BEWARE OF DUMB MUTT
© 2001 PAWS, INC. All Rights Reserved.
HIGH-TECH MIXED BREED
BEWARE OF
Distributed by Universal Press Syndicate
NO THREAT THERE
Beware of Poochie
JIM DAVIS 6-10
I BELIEVE WE HAVE A WINNER

YOU'D NEVER GUESS YOU WERE GOING TO BE 23. WHY, YOU'RE AS ACTIVE AS YOU EVER WERE
www.garfield.com Distributed by Universal Press Syndicate
HA, HA, VERY FUNNY!
JIM DAVIS 6-11
© 2001 PAWS, INC. All Rights Reserved.

SO YOU'LL BE A YEAR OLDER... SO WHAT?
JIM DAVIS 6-12
www.garfield.com Distributed by Universal Press Syndicate
BIRTHDAYS ARE A CELEBRATION OF LIFE!
YEAH, WE CAN DECORATE YOUR WALKER WITH STREAMERS AND EVERYTHING!
WHO LET HIM IN?!!
© 2001 PAWS, INC. All Rights Reserved.

GARFIELD, WILL YOU PLAY WITH ME?
GO AWAY, NERMAL
JIM DAVIS 6-13
www.garfield.com Distributed by Universal Press Syndicate
WE COULD RUN AND LAUGH!
GO AWAY, NERMAL
OR IN YOUR CASE, WADDLE AND WHEEZE
COME CLOSER, NERMAL
© 2001 PAWS, INC. All Rights Reserved.

LOOK ON THE BRIGHT SIDE, GARFIELD...
EVERY YEAR, YOUR BIRTHDAY IS A GIFT!
YEAH, YEAH
A GIFT WITH NO EXCHANGES OR RETURNS
JIM DAVIS 6-14
www.garfield.com Distributed by Universal Press Syndicate
© 2001 PAWS, INC. All Rights Reserved.

I HEAR YOU HAVE A BIRTHDAY COMING UP...HOW OLD?
23
WHAT WOULD THAT BE IN SPIDER YEARS?
DON'T KNOW... NO SPIDER HAS EVER LIVED THAT LONG
WHOA, HOW IRONIC WAS **THAT?**
www.garfield.com Distributed by Universal Press Syndicate
© 2001 PAWS, INC. All Rights Reserved.
JIM DAVIS 6-15

INSTEAD OF MAKING A LIST OF THINGS I WANT FOR MY BIRTHDAY...
I MADE A LIST OF THINGS I **DON'T** WANT
RAISINS?
JIM DAVIS 6-16
www.garfield.com Distributed by Universal Press Syndicate
© 2001 PAWS, INC. All Rights Reserved.

GARFIELD ®
YOU'RE ONLY AS YOUNG AS YOU FEEL, PAL!
SNAP!
Distributed by Universal Press Syndicate
A KITTY TREAT!
www.garfield.com
CRICK SNAP
© 2001 PAWS, INC. All Rights Reserved.
JIM DAVIS 6-17
AND TODAY I FEEL AROUND A HUNDRED AND SIXTY-ONE

SIGH... TOMORROW I'M TURNING 23...
Distributed by Universal Press Syndicate www.garfield.com
DON'T GET ME WRONG... I LOVE BIRTHDAYS
© 2001 PAWS, INC. All Rights Reserved.
JIM DAVIS 6-18
BUT WHY DO SO MANY OF THEM HAVE TO BE MINE ?!

IT'S MY BIRTHDAY AND I GET TO DO ANYTHING I WANT!
JIM DAVIS 6-19
Distributed by Universal Press Syndicate www.garfield.com
...DON'T WAKE ME!
© 2001 PAWS, INC. All Rights Reserved.
WHEE...
Z

GARFIELD, GET OUT OF THAT BED! WHERE'S YOUR SENSE OF WONDER?
Distributed by Universal Press Syndicate www.garfield.com
WHERE'S YOUR SENSE OF ADVENTURE?
© 2001 PAWS, INC. All Rights Reserved.
THEY RAN OFF WITH MY SENSE OF HUMOR
JIM DAVIS 6-20

YOU DIDN'T EAT THAT HAMBURGER?
© 2001 PAWS, INC. All Rights Reserved.
Distributed by Universal Press Syndicate
www.garfield.com
I'M SO PROUD OF YOU
JIM DAVIS 6-21
WELL, I'M AFRAID ODIE'S A LITTLE DISAPPOINTED IN YOU
SQUEAK SQUEAK SQUEAK

Z
Distributed by Universal Press Syndicate
www.garfield.com
IT'S NICE WHEN GARFIELD'S ASLEEP. HE CAN'T ANNOY ME
Z
© 2001 PAWS, INC. All Rights Reserved.
Z
JIM DAVIS 6-22

STEP RIGHT THIS WAY, LADIES AND GENTLEMEN
JIM DAVIS 6-23
GARFIELD
Distributed by Universal Press Syndicate
www.garfield.com
HERE WE HAVE ONE OF NATURE'S WONDERS
GARFIELD
© 2001 PAWS, INC. All Rights Reserved.
THE BOTTOMLESS PIT
I WANT TO BE LEFT ALONE
GARFIELD

GARFIELD®
www.garfield.com
THESE ARE THE DAYS THAT I LOVE
Distributed by Universal Press Syndicate
DAYS WHEN YOU CAN LIE IN ONE SPOT FROM SUNRISE TO SUNSET, WHILE ABSOLUTELY NOTHING HAPPENS
NO CRISES, NO ACCOMPLISHMENTS, NO NOTHING
JUST YOURSELF AND A QUIET, SERENE, AND PEACEFUL DAY
JIM DAVIS 6·24
© 2001 PAWS, INC. All Rights Reserved.
HE FOLLOWED ME HOME. CAN I KEEP HIM?
I JUST COULDN'T LEAVE WELL ENOUGH ALONE

IT'S COMEDY TIME!
JIM DAVIS 6-25
Distributed by Universal Press Syndicate www.garfield.com
AM I THE ONLY ONE WHO THINKS BOW TIES ARE FUNNY?!
© 2001 PAWS, INC. All Rights Reserved.

I SHALL NOW MAKE MY ASSISTANT DISAPPEAR
Distributed by Universal Press Syndicate www.garfield.com
BOOT!
© 2001 PAWS, INC. All Rights Reserved. JIM DAVIS 6-26
NOT VERY MAGICAL, BUT PRETTY ENTERTAINING!
THUD!

A FUNNY THING HAPPENED ON THE WAY TO THE FENCE TONIGHT...
Distributed by Universal Press Syndicate www.garfield.com
ALL RIGHT!
© 2001 PAWS, INC. All Rights Reserved. JIM DAVIS 6-27
YEAH! LET'S GO THERE!
I HATE YOU ALL

SO, ANYBODY HERE FROM OUT OF TOWN?
YES, I AM FROM THE PLANET URANUS
ENTERTAIN ME OR DIE, EARTHLING!
I HATE THESE LATE SHOWS
JIM DAVIS 6-28
Distributed by Universal Press Syndicate www.garfield.com
© 2001 PAWS, INC. All Rights Reserved.

WHO WANTS TO HEAR A SONG?
I DO!
ME TOO!
SURE!
ANY REQUESTS?
TURN ON THE RADIO!
YEAH!
THAT WOULD BE GREAT!
JIM DAVIS 6-29
Distributed by Universal Press Syndicate www.garfield.com
© 2001 PAWS, INC. All Rights Reserved.

HOW DO YOU LIKE THE SHOW SO FAR?
Z Z Z Z Z Z
ALL RIGHT! A STANDING NAP!
Z Z Z Z Z Z Z
JIM DAVIS 6-30
Distributed by Universal Press Syndicate www.garfield.com
© 2001 PAWS, INC. All Rights Reserved.

GARFIELD
R
Distributed by Universal Press Syndicate
SLUP
www.garfield.com
© 2001 PAWS, INC. All Rights Reserved.
JIGGITTA JIGGITTA JIGGITTA JIGGITTA
ZORK
FFFFNNNNNNNNNNNN
NONG NONG NONG NONG NONG NONG
A LITTLE ESPRESSO GOES A LONG WAY
JIM DAVIS 7-1

CRASH!
CRASH! CRASH! CRASH! CRASH!
THAT ODIE IS NO PLATE CATCHER
I HEAR NOTHING...
JIM DAVIS 7-2
www.garfield.com Distributed by Universal Press Syndicate
© 2001 PAWS, INC. All Rights Reserved.

YOU KNOW, MOST CATS DON'T GET TO HAVE ICE CREAM
ALL RIGHT!
ALL THE MORE FOR ME!
JIM DAVIS 7-3
www.garfield.com Distributed by Universal Press Syndicate
© 2001 PAWS, INC. All Rights Reserved.

YOU SEEM CONTENT, JON
LOOKS LIKE I GOT HERE JUST IN TIME
GO AWAY, GARFIELD
I'M HERE TO SUCK THE JOY OUT OF YOUR LIFE
JIM DAVIS 7-4
www.garfield.com Distributed by Universal Press Syndicate
© 2001 PAWS, INC. All Rights Reserved.

ODIE SURE IS ENJOYING THAT RAWHIDE CHEW I GAVE HIM
I CAN'T FIND MY NEW BELT
THAT EXPLAINS THE BUCKLE
www.garfield.com
Distributed by Universal Press Syndicate
© 2001 PAWS, INC. All Rights Reserved.
JIM DAVIS 7-5

I FEED JON'S CANARY EVERY DAY
IT'S A SELFLESS ACT ON MY PART
BUT SOON IT WILL BE HARVEST TIME
www.garfield.com
Distributed by Universal Press Syndicate
© 2001 PAWS, INC. All Rights Reserved.
JIM DAVIS 7-6

DOES THIS OUTFIT MAKE ME LOOK MYSTERIOUS?
ABSOLUTELY!
I THINK DORKS ARE VERY MYSTERIOUS
www.garfield.com
Distributed by Universal Press Syndicate
© 2001 PAWS, INC. All Rights Reserved.
JIM DAVIS 7-7

Garfield
JIM DAVIS 7-8
Distributed by Universal Press Syndicate
BEWARE OF DOG
BEWARE OF DOG
BEWARE OF DOG
BEWARE OF DOG
www.garfield.com
WHOOMP
TREEE DOOOOG!
BEWARE OF

SPIDERS WERE NOT MEANT TO BE SQUISHED! WE ARE FEELING, LIVING BEINGS! WE ARE–
www.garfield.com
Distributed by Universal Press Syndicate
SOMEBODY GRAB A HOUSE SLIPPER, QUICK!
© 2001 PAWS, INC. All Rights Reserved.
JIM DAVIS 7-9

SO, I SEE YOU HAVE A WALKING CAST NOW
YEAH
www.garfield.com
Distributed by Universal Press Syndicate
I'D ASK YOU TO SIGN IT, BUT I HATE YOUR STINKING GUTS, YOU FAT TUB OF LARD!
© 2001 PAWS, INC. All Rights Reserved.
JIM DAVIS 7-10

YOU MAY SQUISH ME, BUT YOU'LL NEVER SQUISH MY SPIRIT!
JIM DAVIS 7-11
www.garfield.com
Distributed by Universal Press Syndicate
KER
SMACK
HOW'S YOUR SPIRIT, STEWART?
BITE ME, MIKEY
© 2001 PAWS, INC. All Rights Reserved.

I WANT YOU TO SQUISH MY LOUSY NO-GOOD HUSBAND!
www.garfield.com
Distributed by Universal Press Syndicate
THEN I WANT YOU TO POUND HIM INTO MULCH, AND THEN RIP HIS LEGS OFF AND STUFF THEM DOWN HIS CRAW!
© 2001 PAWS, INC. All Rights Reserved.
HE GAVE YOU VACUUM CLEANER BAGS FOR YOUR WEDDING ANNIVERSARY AGAIN, DIDN'T HE?
**CANISTER** BAGS!...AND I HAVE AN UPRIGHT!
JIM DAVIS
7-12

HAVE YOU SEEN MY SISTER?
JIM DAVIS 7-13
www.garfield.com
Distributed by Universal Press Syndicate
SMACKO
© 2001 PAWS, INC. All Rights Reserved.
HAVE YOU SEEN MY BROTHER?
I THINK SO. DOES HE LOOK LIKE THIS?

SEE THE CAT TODAY?
YEP
JIM DAVIS 7-14
www.garfield.com
Distributed by Universal Press Syndicate
AND HE **DIDN'T** SQUISH YOU?!
OH, SURE HE DID
© 2001 PAWS, INC. All Rights Reserved.
THIS IS A BLACK BODY CAST
DONK DONK

GARFIELD®
www.garfield.com
GARFIELD...
I WOULDN'T KEEP TEASING THE DOG IN THAT PICKUP
JIM DAVIS 7-15
Distributed by Universal Press Syndicate
YOU NEVER KNOW WHEN WE MIGHT COME TO A RED LIGHT
© 2001 PAWS, INC. All Rights Reserved.
LIKE THIS ONE

CATS ARE VERY COMPLICATED
YOU'RE A LUMP
CATS ARE VERY COMPLICATED LUMPS
JIM DAVIS 7-16
www.garfield.com Distributed by Universal Press Syndicate
© 2001 PAWS, INC. All Rights Reserved.

SAYS HERE A CAT WILL ALWAYS LAND ON ITS FEET
JIM DAVIS 7-17
© 2001 PAWS, INC. All Rights Reserved.
RIIIGHT
I SUBSCRIBE TO THE "BOUNCE" SCHOOL OF THOUGHT
Distributed by Universal Press Syndicate www.garfield.com

JON'S ICED TEA
JIM DAVIS 7-18
© 2001 PAWS, INC. All Rights Reserved.
FLICK
A LA GARFIELD
Distributed by Universal Press Syndicate www.garfield.com

I'LL GO GET THE BROOM...
JIM DAVIS 7-19
© 2001 PAWS, INC. All Rights Reserved.
AND SWEEP UP ALL THAT CAT HAIR
OKAY, BUT FIRST...
www.garfield.com Distributed by Universal Press Syndicate
I'D JUST LIKE TO STAND HERE AND ADMIRE IT AWHILE

YOU KNOW WHAT I LOVE ABOUT CATS, GARFIELD? YOU'RE SO REFINED...
© 2001 PAWS, INC. All Rights Reserved.
HAAAACK!!
Distributed by Universal Press Syndicate www.garfield.com
AHEM... YOU WERE SAYING?
JIM DAVIS 7-20

LIFE OFFERS US MANY CHALLENGES
© 2001 PAWS, INC. All Rights Reserved.
AND THAT'S WHY I'M GOING TO HIDE BEHIND THE COUCH
Distributed by Universal Press Syndicate www.garfield.com
DON'T TELL LIFE
JIM DAVIS 7-21

Garfield®
Distributed by Universal Press Syndicate
© 2001 PAWS, INC. All Rights Reserved.
www.garfield.com
CAN YOU PLEASE SPEED IT UP A LITTLE?!
FLEA DIP DAY
JIM DAVIS 7-22

I AM A MAGIC DONUT!
I CAN GRANT YOU ANY WISH!
HOW ABOUT A GLASS OF MILK?
JIM DAVIS 7-23
Distributed by Universal Press Syndicate www.garfield.com
© 2001 PAWS, INC. All Rights Reserved.

ALL OF US HAVE A DESTINY, GARFIELD
I WONDER WHAT MY PLACE IN HISTORY WILL BE?
SOMEWHERE BETWEEN FLOYD THE WHISTLING SNAKE AND CRAB GRASS
JIM DAVIS 7-24
www.garfield.com Distributed by Universal Press Syndicate
© 2001 PAWS, INC. All Rights Reserved.

ODIE IS TRYING TO ANNOY ME
HE'S MAKING THAT NOISE I HATE
THAT CONTINUOUS BREATHING SOUND
JIM DAVIS 7-25
Distributed by Universal Press Syndicate www.garfield.com
© 2001 PAWS, INC. All Rights Reserved.

DO YOU EVER STOP TO REALIZE ALL YOU PUT ME THROUGH?!
YOU KNOW, I NEVER DID!
JIM DAVIS 7-26
Distributed by Universal Press Syndicate www.garfield.com
© 2001 PAWS, INC. All Rights Reserved.

I'VE TRIED EVERY GIRL IN MY ADDRESS BOOK EXCEPT LORETTA GNISH
JIM DAVIS 7-27
I WONDER IF SHE EVER HAD SURGERY TO REMOVE THAT THIRD NOSTRIL?
HE'S WEAKENING
Distributed by Universal Press Syndicate www.garfield.com
© 2001 PAWS, INC. All Rights Reserved.

YOU FORGOT MY BIRTHDAY
JIM DAVIS 7-28
NO, I DIDN'T
I DIDN'T CARE!
Distributed by Universal Press Syndicate www.garfield.com
© 2001 PAWS, INC. All Rights Reserved.

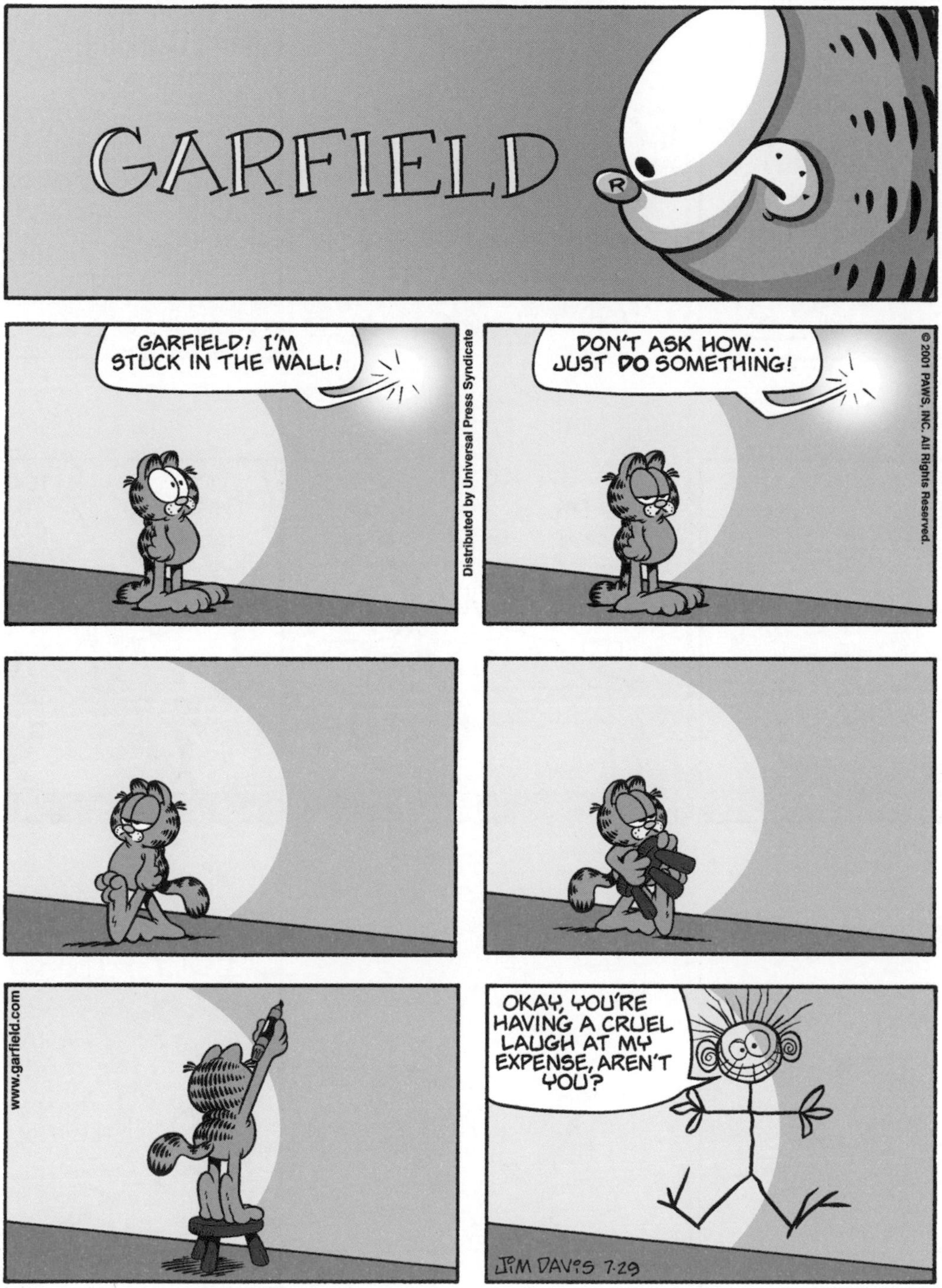
GARFIELD
GARFIELD! I'M STUCK IN THE WALL!
Distributed by Universal Press Syndicate
DON'T ASK HOW... JUST DO SOMETHING!
© 2001 PAWS, INC. All Rights Reserved.
www.garfield.com
OKAY, YOU'RE HAVING A CRUEL LAUGH AT MY EXPENSE, AREN'T YOU?
JIM DAVIS 7-29

DID YOU BRING THE PAPER IN?
JIM DAVIS 7-30
www.garfield.com
Distributed by Universal Press Syndicate
GARFIELD!
KIDDING! I SAVED THE FUNNIES!
© 2001 PAWS, INC. All Rights Reserved.

I WONDER WHAT TIME IT IS?
www.garfield.com
Distributed by Universal Press Syndicate
OW! OW! OW!
IT'S THREE
TOO CLOSE TO THE CUCKOO CLOCK
JIM DAVIS 7-31
© 2001 PAWS, INC. All Rights Reserved.

JIM DAVIS 8-1
www.garfield.com
Distributed by Universal Press Syndicate
♪FEEELINGS...
WHAT IS A KARAOKE MACHINE DOING IN THE LIVING ROOM?
© 2001 PAWS, INC. All Rights Reserved.

AAAAGGGHHH
WHO TORE THE LAST PAGE OUT OF THE MYSTERY BOOK I WAS READING?!
THE CAT DID IT
JIM DAVIS 8-2
Distributed by Universal Press Syndicate www.garfield.com
© 2001 PAWS, INC. All Rights Reserved.

I WALKED MY DATE TO HER DOOR
AND THEN WHAT HAPPENED?
I KISSED HER HAND...
AND THEN WHAT HAPPENED?
LEAVING HER OTHER HAND FREE...
AND THEN WHAT HAPPENED?
JIM DAVIS 8-3
Distributed by Universal Press Syndicate www.garfield.com
© 2001 PAWS, INC. All Rights Reserved.

I SAT ON A BEE TODAY
SO I'M NOT HAPPY
I'LL BET THE BEE ISN'T EXACTLY GLEEFUL, EITHER
JIM DAVIS 8-4
Distributed by Universal Press Syndicate www.garfield.com
© 2001 PAWS, INC. All Rights Reserved.

GARFIELD®
www.garfield.com
SPIDERS ARE YOUR FRIEEEEEEENDS...
Z
Distributed by Universal Press Syndicate
YOU LIIIIIIIIKE SPIDERS
Z
YOU WOULD NEVVVVVVVVVVER HURT A SPIDER...
Z
NEXT MORNING:
MORNING, FRIEND!
SMACK!
I'M A LIIIIIIIGHT SLEEEEEEPER
© 2001 PAWS, INC. All Rights Reserved.
JIM DAVIS 8-5

JIM DAVIS 8-6
www.garfield.com
Distributed by Universal Press Syndicate
TAH DAH!
© 2001 PAWS, INC. All Rights Reserved.

BARK! BARK!
www.garfield.com
Distributed by Universal Press Syndicate
DOG TREAT
JIM DAVIS 8-7
© 2001 PAWS, INC. All Rights Reserved.
YEH! YEH! YEH! YEH!
THEY'RE SO EASY

TONIGHT WE HAVE WITH US A MAN WHO THINKS HE'S A DOG...HOW ARE YOU, SIR?
www.garfield.com
Distributed by Universal Press Syndicate
DOGS CAN'T TALK, PHIL
BUT YOU JUST DID
© 2001 PAWS, INC. All Rights Reserved.
UH...I MEAN, "ARF"
PEOPLE WILL DO ANYTHING TO GET ON TV
JIM DAVIS 8-8

THE TOASTER DOESN'T WORK, GARFIELD
www.garfield.com
Distributed by Universal Press Syndicate
I'LL TAKE IT TO THE GARAGE AND FIX IT
NOT THE GARAGE!
© 2001 PAWS, INC. All Rights Reserved.
THAT'S WHERE ALL SMALL APPLIANCES GO TO DIE
JIM DAVIS 8-9

I KNOW WHY YOU WON'T GO OUT WITH ME, CINDY
JIM DAVIS 8-10
www.garfield.com
Distributed by Universal Press Syndicate
YOU THINK I'M STUPID, DON'T YOU?...
© 2001 PAWS, INC. All Rights Reserved.
DARN, I WAS HOPING THAT WASN'T IT
YOU WERE HOPING FOR "LOSER," MAYBE?

DING-DONG
www.garfield.com
Distributed by Universal Press Syndicate
SQUEEK SQUEEK SQUEEK SQUEEK SQUEEK
© 2001 PAWS, INC. All Rights Reserved.
WHO WAS IT?
JUST SOME CLOWN
JIM DAVIS 8-11

GARFIELD®
IF YOU WANT A COOKIE, YOU'LL HAVE TO MOVE
Distributed by Universal Press Syndicate
© 2001 PAWS, INC. All Rights Reserved.
www.garfield.com
I FORGOT HOW FAR CATS CAN STRETCH
NOW, I THINK I'LL GET SOME MILK OUT OF OUR NEIGHBOR'S REFRIGERATOR
JIM DAVIS 8·12

MOM USED TO TUCK ME INTO BED AT NIGHT
JIM DAVIS 8-13
www.garfield.com
Distributed by Universal Press Syndicate
SHE'D KISS ME ON THE FOREHEAD AND SAY, "NIGHTY-NIGHT"
© 2001 PAWS, INC. All Rights Reserved.
THEN DAD WOULD TIPTOE IN AND WHISPER, "BEWARE THE CHICKEN!"
I'VE ALWAYS LIKED YOUR DAD

LOOK, GARFIELD! A PACKAGE FROM MY MOM!
I WONDER WHAT IT IS?!
© 2001 PAWS, INC. All Rights Reserved.
Distributed by Universal Press Syndicate
www.garfield.com
I HOPE IT'S COOKIES!
I HOPE IT'S A HAM!
JIM DAVIS 8-14
IT'S HAM-SHAPED COOKIES!
MOM SHOOTS! MOM **SCORES!**

WE COULDN'T AFFORD DOCTORS ON THE FARM
JIM DAVIS 8-15
www.garfield.com
Distributed by Universal Press Syndicate
WE RELIED ON NATURAL REMEDIES
© 2001 PAWS, INC. All Rights Reserved.
DID YOU KNOW THAT KISSING A CHICKEN CURES COLD SORES?
GET AWAY FROM ME

NEWS FROM THE FARM, GARFIELD... A LETTER FROM DOC BOY
JIM DAVIS 8-16
www.garfield.com
Distributed by Universal Press Syndicate
"MADDIE FERGUSON'S PIE TOOK FIRST PLACE AT THE FAIR..."
© 2001 PAWS, INC. All Rights Reserved.
"SO MOM BURNED HER BARN DOWN"
ALL RIGHT, MOM!

GARFIELD IS FINE, MOM...WANT TO TALK TO HIM?
JIM DAVIS 8-17
www.garfield.com
Distributed by Universal Press Syndicate
© 2001 PAWS, INC. All Rights Reserved.
WHAT'S SHE SAYING?
SHE'S SAYING SHE CAN'T BELIEVE SHE'S TALKING TO A CAT ON A LONG-DISTANCE CALL

WE GOT A POST CARD FROM DOC BOY!
www.garfield.com
Distributed by Universal Press Syndicate
HE'S VACATIONING IN LOOGIEVILLE, INDIANA
© 2001 PAWS, INC. All Rights Reserved.
...SAYS HE HAD HIS PICTURE TAKEN WITH THE WORLD'S LARGEST CORN COB
EIFFEL TOWER, EAT YOUR HEART OUT
JIM DAVIS 8-18

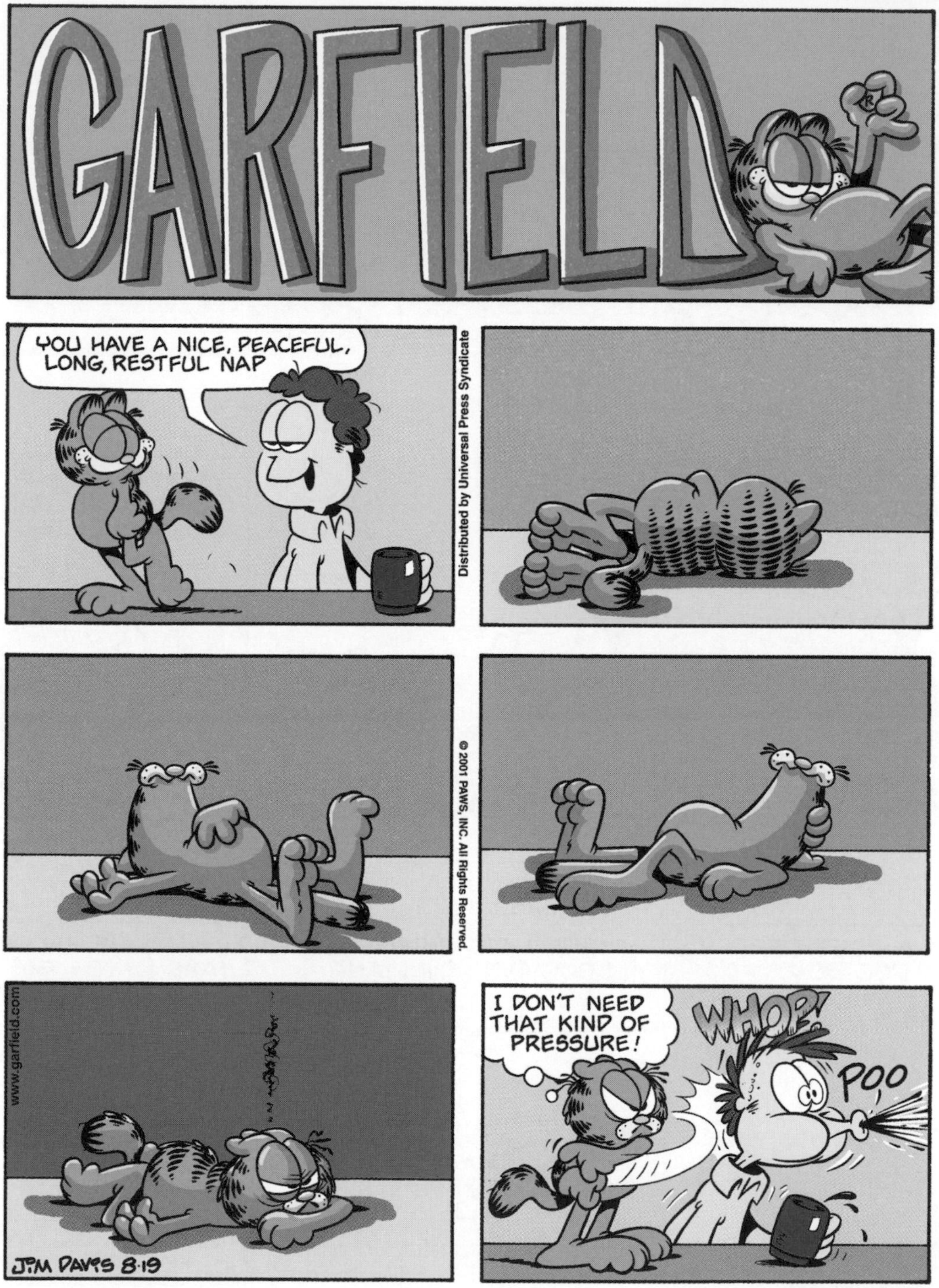
GARFIELD
YOU HAVE A NICE, PEACEFUL, LONG, RESTFUL NAP
Distributed by Universal Press Syndicate
© 2001 PAWS, INC. All Rights Reserved.
www.garfield.com
JIM DAVIS 8-19
I DON'T NEED THAT KIND OF PRESSURE!
WHOP!
POO

I'VE DECIDED TO DO NOTHING... JUST LIKE YOU
GOOD LUCK, PAL
NOBODY CAN DO NOTHING LIKE ME
JIM DAVIS 8-20
Distributed by Universal Press Syndicate www.garfield.com
© 2001 PAWS, INC. All Rights Reserved.

GARFIELD, I FOUND A TREASURE
A RECORD ALBUM?
IT'S A CLASSIC
"MEL TWEEDY'S BEST FARM TUNES"?
IT HAS ALL THE HITS!
"OUR LOVE'S GONE DRY AND SO HAS THE COW"
Mel Tweedy
JIM DAVIS 8-21
Distributed by Universal Press Syndicate www.garfield.com
© 2001 PAWS, INC. All Rights Reserved.

I LEARN FROM MY MISTAKES
WOW
THERE GOES THE WORLD'S SMARTEST MAN!
JIM DAVIS 8-22
Distributed by Universal Press Syndicate www.garfield.com
© 2001 PAWS, INC. All Rights Reserved.

JIM DAVIS 8-23
www.garfield.com
Distributed by Universal Press Syndicate
PANT
PANT
PANT
© 2001 PAWS, INC. All Rights Reserved.
LEATHER BREATH
HEY! WHERE'S MY OTHER SHOE?!

I BOUGHT THIS BOX OF CANDY FOR MY DATE!
www.garfield.com
Distributed by Universal Press Syndicate
AND I ATE IT
© 2001 PAWS, INC. All Rights Reserved.
JIM DAVIS 8-24
WE'RE A TEAM!

WELL, THE DISHES ARE WASHED
www.garfield.com
Distributed by Universal Press Syndicate
© 2001 PAWS, INC. All Rights Reserved.
MAYBE I'LL WAX THEM
IT'S THE WEEKEND THAT WOULDN'T END
JIM DAVIS 8-25

Garfield®
IS A BIG FAT
AH HA!
www.garfield.com
OH. YOU'RE NOT DOING ANYTHING
Distributed by Universal Press Syndicate
AH HA!
OH. YOU'RE STILL NOT DOING ANYTHING
© 2001 PAWS, INC. All Rights Reserved.
AH HA!
I'LL LET YOU KNOW
JIM DAVIS 8-26

I THINK I'LL TAKE A NAP
JIM DAVIS 8-27
THEN DOZE AWHILE...AND THEN TOP IT ALL OFF WITH A NICE SNOOZE
REMEMBER, KIDS, FOR WELL-BALANCED REST, YOU MUST HAVE SOMETHING FROM THE THREE BASIC SLEEP GROUPS EACH DAY
Distributed by Universal Press Syndicate www.garfield.com
© 2001 PAWS, INC. All Rights Reserved.

HMF!
IF YOU CONTINUE TO LIE THERE LIKE THAT, YOU'RE GOING TO ATROPHY!
I'D GO TO THE DICTIONARY TO LOOK THAT UP, BUT MY LEGS HAVE WITHERED
JIM DAVIS 8-28
Distributed by Universal Press Syndicate www.garfield.com
© 2001 PAWS, INC. All Rights Reserved.

I'M BORED
REEEALLY BORED
I'M SO BORED IT'S ALMOST INTERESTING
JIM DAVIS 8-29
Distributed by Universal Press Syndicate www.garfield.com
© 2001 PAWS, INC. All Rights Reserved.

MAYBE THERE **IS** SOMETHING TO LYING ON YOUR BACK...MAYBE I SHOULD TRY IT
Distributed by Universal Press Syndicate www.garfield.com
JIM DAVIS 8·30
© 2001 PAWS, INC. All Rights Reserved.
LOOK AT ALL THE **GUM** STUCK UNDER THIS TABLE!
CLOSE YOUR EYES, DIPWAD

I'M GOING OUT FOR A WHILE
JIM DAVIS 8·31
Distributed by Universal Press Syndicate www.garfield.com
DON'T BOTHER WAITING...
© 2001 PAWS, INC. All Rights Reserved.
Z
...UP FOR ME

THAT'S WHAT YOU WERE DOING LAST TIME I SAW YOU!
Distributed by Universal Press Syndicate www.garfield.com
© 2001 PAWS, INC. All Rights Reserved.
I'M A RERUN
JIM DAVIS 9·1

Garfield
WELCOME TO "COLLEGIATE FACE SLAPPING"!
GOOD LUCK, GENTLEMEN. SHAKE HANDS AND COME OUT SLAPPING!
DING
SLAP SLAP SLAP SLAP SLAPPY SLAPPY SLAP SLAP SLAPPITY SLAPPITY SLAP*POINK*
UH-OH! WE HAVE A PENALTY FLAG
SO SORRY, CONTESTANT NUMBER ONE, BUT YOUR LAST SLAP WAS, IN FACT, AN EYE POINK
TWO POINTS OFF...
TWO POINTS?! THAT WASN'T AN EYE POINK! HERE'S AN EYE POINK!
POINK
AND THE REF GOES DOWN!
WHAT DID WE EVER DO BEFORE 32 SPORTS CHANNELS?
JIM DAVIS 9-2
Distributed by Universal Press Syndicate
© 2001 PAWS, INC. All Rights Reserved.

GARFIELD, WHAT'S WRONG WITH THIS PICTURE?
GARFIELD
www.garfield.com Distributed by Universal Press Syndicate
© 2001 PAWS, INC. All Rights Reserved.
JIM DAVIS 9-3

www.garfield.com Distributed by Universal Press Syndicate
BOY, IT'S BORING IN HERE!
© 2001 PAWS, INC. All Rights Reserved.
I COULDN'T HAVE DONE IT WITHOUT YOU, ODIE
JIM DAVIS 9-4

CRUNCH
www.garfield.com Distributed by Universal Press Syndicate
CRUNCH CRUNCH CRU
CRUNCH CRUNCH CRUN
© 2001 PAWS, INC. All Rights Reserved.
JIM DAVIS 9-5
TIME TO GO GROCERY SHOPPING, GARFIELD
SUGAR CUBE SANDWICH

BARK! BARK! BARK!
JIM DAVIS 9·6
www.garfield.com
GUM?
© 2001 PAWS, INC. All Rights Reserved.
MMMB! MMMB! MMMB!
I LOVE DOGS
Distributed by Universal Press Syndicate

IT'S THE WEEKEND
JIM DAVIS 9·7
www.garfield.com
Distributed by Universal Press Syndicate
BOREDOM IS AT THE DOOR
© 2001 PAWS, INC. All Rights Reserved.
HEY, WATERMELON SEEDS STICK TO YOUR FACE!
AND WALKS RIGHT IN WITHOUT KNOCKING

I'M GOING TO SHOW ELLEN MY INTELLECTUAL SIDE
www.garfield.com
Distributed by Universal Press Syndicate
I'M WRITING A LIST OF BOOKS I'VE READ
© 2001 PAWS, INC. All Rights Reserved.
"DUCKY'S BIG POND"?
NO PICTURES IN THAT ONE, PAL!
JIM DAVIS 9·8

Garfield®
I JUST PASSED MRS. FEENY ON THE SIDEWALK
HER ARM WAS IN A SLING. SHE WAS WEARING A NECK BRACE
SHE HAD A WALKING CAST...
AND HER JAW WAS WIRED SHUT
SHE GAVE ME A VERY NASTY LOOK
YOU WOULDN'T KNOW ANYTHING ABOUT THIS, WOULD YOU?
NO, AND I DON'T KNOW WHAT HAPPENED TO YOUR BALL BEARING COLLECTION, EITHER
JIM DAVIS 9-9
www.garfield.com
Distributed by Universal Press Syndicate
© 2001 PAWS, INC. All Rights Reserved.

CLICK CLICK
HE WHAT?!
JIM DAVIS 9-10
www.garfield.com
Distributed by Universal Press Syndicate
COULD YOU HOLD FOR A MOMENT? I HAVE ANOTHER CALL COMING IN... THANKS
*BOOP*
© 2001 PAWS, INC. All Rights Reserved.
HE WHAT?!
I'VE BEEN A BUSY BOY

WE ALL HAVE TO LIVE TOGETHER
www.garfield.com
Distributed by Universal Press Syndicate
WE HAVE TO BE CONSIDERATE OF OUR NEIGHBORS
© 2001 PAWS, INC. All Rights Reserved.
SO RETURN THOSE TO MRS. FEENY!
CAN I KEEP THE PEARLS?
JIM DAVIS 9-11

MRS. FEENY'S LITTLE DOG IS MISSING AGAIN...
www.garfield.com
Distributed by Universal Press Syndicate
AND ALL THOSE STAMPS I BOUGHT YESTERDAY ARE GONE, NOT TO MENTION A BOX AND SOME TWINE!
© 2001 PAWS, INC. All Rights Reserved.
TAKE YOUR TIME... IT'LL COME TO YOU
JIM DAVIS 9-12

DEAL?
DEAL
JIM DAVIS 9-13
www.garfield.com
Distributed by Universal Press Syndicate
WHERE WAS THAT MOUSE GOING WITH A DOLLAR?
TO RUN UP MRS. FEENY'S LEG. MAY I BORROW THE VIDEO CAMERA?
© 2001 PAWS, INC. All Rights Reserved.

WHOCK! SLAP!
GOUGE-GOUGE
SMACK! SMACK! SMACK!
www.garfield.com
Distributed by Universal Press Syndicate
THAT WAS MRS. FEENY AT THE DOOR FOR YOU...
SHE SAID WHEN SHE CATCHES YOU, SHE'S GOING TO DO THIS TO YOU
I THINK I'LL STAY IN TODAY
© 2001 PAWS, INC. All Rights Reserved.
JIM DAVIS 9-14

YOU'LL HAVE TO SPEAK LOUDER, MRS. FEENY! I CAN'T HEAR YOU OVER ALL THAT RACKET!
www.garfield.com
Distributed by Universal Press Syndicate
JIM DAVIS 9-15
HE PUT WHAT?... HOW MANY?!
© 2001 PAWS, INC. All Rights Reserved.
WHERE DID YOU FIND FIFTEEN HOWLER MONKEYS?!
RIIIING
THAT WOULD BE THE ZOO

GARFIELD®
www.garfield.com
DUM, DEE DUM, DEE DUM...
Distributed by Universal Press Syndicate
HI, SPIDER
UH, HI, CAT...
© 2001 PAWS, INC. All Rights Reserved.
PAT PAT PAT
WOW! I MUST BE DREAMING!
STOMP
YAAAHHH!!!
POOOEY!!!
JIM DAVIS 9·16

GARFIELD, WHY DO I KEEP DWELLING ON THE PAST?
JIM DAVIS 9-17
Distributed by Universal Press Syndicate
www.garfield.com
BECAUSE YOU HAVE NO FUTURE?
© 2001 PAWS, INC. All Rights Reserved.
HERE'S MY FIRST POCKET PROTECTOR
AND NO PAST

THERE'S PATTY EVANS, MY DATE FOR THE JUNIOR PROM
JIM DAVIS 9-18
Year Book
Distributed by Universal Press Syndicate
www.garfield.com
I REMEMBER I WAS SO NERVOUS PINNING THE CORSAGE ON HER
© 2001 PAWS, INC. All Rights Reserved.
SHE SAID SHE'LL ALWAYS HAVE THE SCAR TO REMEMBER ME BY
OKAY, LEMME SEE

THAT'S COACH BECK
YEAR Book
Distributed by Universal Press Syndicate
www.garfield.com
HE WAS A TOUGH TOBACCO-CHEWIN' OLD FOOTBALL COACH
© 2001 PAWS, INC. All Rights Reserved.
HE ALWAYS SPIT IN MY HELMET
GOOD THING YOU NEVER USED IT
JIM DAVIS 9-19

"GEEK"...
"LOSER"...
"CREEP"...
"FREAK"...
"DORK BOY"...
"YOU STINK!"
READING THE INSCRIPTIONS IN HIS HIGH SCHOOL YEARBOOK
JPM DAVPS 9·20
Distributed by Universal Press Syndicate www.garfield.com
© 2001 PAWS, INC. All Rights Reserved.

BETH NARDONE, NOW **THERE** WAS A GIRL!
SHE BROKE MY HEART...
**AND** MY JAW
BOY MEETS GIRL, BOY LOSES TEETH
JPM DAVPS 9·21
Distributed by Universal Press Syndicate www.garfield.com
© 2001 PAWS, INC. All Rights Reserved.

BELINDA GILZONE...I HAD A MAD CRUSH ON HER
SHE WAS HEAD CHEERLEADER
EVER HAD AN ENTIRE POMPON SHOVED UP YOUR NOSE?
LET ME THINK .....NO
JPM DAVPS 9·22
Distributed by Universal Press Syndicate www.garfield.com
© 2001 PAWS, INC. All Rights Reserved.

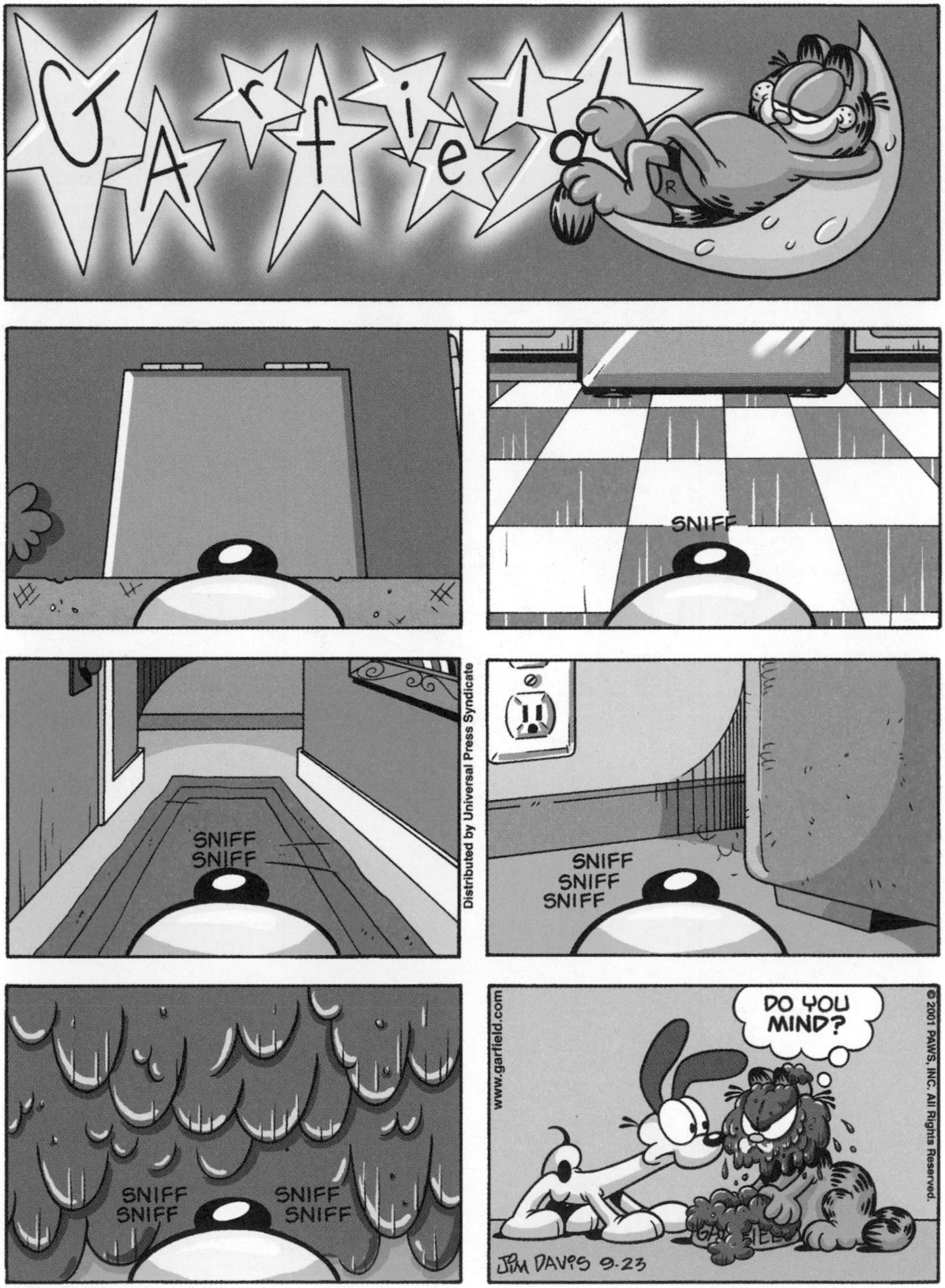
Garfield
SNIFF
SNIFF
SNIFF
SNIFF
SNIFF
SNIFF
SNIFF SNIFF
SNIFF SNIFF
DO YOU MIND?
Distributed by Universal Press Syndicate
www.garfield.com
© 2001 PAWS, INC. All Rights Reserved.
JIM DAVIS 9-23

MONDAYS DON'T SCARE ME...
TOiiiiiiiiNG
FOOMP
OH, SURE, THEY CHEESE ME OFF, BUT THEY DON'T SCARE ME
JIM DAVIS 9-24
www.garfield.com
Distributed by Universal Press Syndicate
© 2001 PAWS, INC. All Rights Reserved.

FUN WITH TAPE!
JIM DAVIS 9-25
www.garfield.com
Distributed by Universal Press Syndicate
© 2001 PAWS, INC. All Rights Reserved.

MORNING
MORNING
SIP
SO, WHAT'S IT LIKE TO LICK A SPARK PLUG?
JIM DAVIS 9-26
www.garfield.com
Distributed by Universal Press Syndicate
© 2001 PAWS, INC. All Rights Reserved.

CATS ARE PRIMAL, JON
JIM DAVIS 9-27
www.garfield.com
Distributed by Universal Press Syndicate
I HAVE THE URGE TO PROWL
© 2001 PAWS, INC. All Rights Reserved.
GO AWAY
GIMME YOUR CAR KEYS

YAWN
SCRATCH SCRATCH
© 2001 PAWS, INC. All Rights Reserved.
JIM DAVIS 9-28
BURP
www.garfield.com
Distributed by Universal Press Syndicate
SHE SEEMED NICE

SNIFF SNIFF
© 2001 PAWS, INC. All Rights Reserved.
WHAT SMELLS SO GOOD?
CREAM OF CANARY
Distributed by Universal Press Syndicate
www.garfield.com
CHUNKY STYLE
JIM DAVIS 9-29

GARFIELD
THAT WAS MRS. FEENY AGAIN
DO TELL
WHY DO YOU TORTURE THAT WOMAN SO?
BECAUSE SHE'S THERE
www.garfield.com
...HIDING HER DENTURES?!
SHE BITES WHEN SHE'S ANGRY
© 2001 PAWS, INC. All Rights Reserved.
SNEAKING HER LITTLE DOG LAXATIVE-LACED BRAN MUFFINS?!
WHAT'S SO IRREGULAR ABOUT THAT?
...SOAPING HER CAR WINDOWS WITH THE WORDS "FEENY IS A WEENIE"?!!
YOU KNOW I CAN'T SPELL... I PAID A KID TO DO THAT!
Distributed by Universal Press Syndicate
WHAT AM I GOING TO DO WITH YOU?!
RELAX...HERE, HAVE A BRAN MUFFIN
JIM DAVIS 9-30

HEY, JON!
Distributed by Universal Press Syndicate www.garfield.com
LOOK AT ME!
I'M IN THREE ROOMS AT THE SAME TIME!
© 2001 PAWS, INC. All Rights Reserved.
DIET TIME!
JIM DAVIS 10-1

YOU'RE FAT
Distributed by Universal Press Syndicate www.garfield.com
NO, NO, I AM BIG BONED
© 2001 PAWS, INC. All Rights Reserved.
JIM DAVIS 10-2
GODZILLA WAS BIG BONED... YOU'RE FAT

NO MORE SNACKS FOR YOU, GARFIELD
FINE
JIM DAVIS 10-3
Distributed by Universal Press Syndicate www.garfield.com
YOU ARE ON A STRICT DIET
WHATEVER YOU SAY
© 2001 PAWS, INC. All Rights Reserved.
AND I FILLED IN THE TUNNEL TO THE REFRIGERATOR
MY LIFE IS OVER

IT'S NOT THE DIETING THAT GETS TO ME
www.garfield.com
Distributed by Universal Press Syndicate
© 2001 PAWS, INC. All Rights Reserved.
IT'S THE NOT EATING PART!!!
JIM DAVIS 10.4

AREN'T YOU GOING TO EAT YOUR DINNER?
www.garfield.com
Distributed by Universal Press Syndicate
I'M DECIDING
© 2001 PAWS, INC. All Rights Reserved.
I MAY JUST WEEP INSTEAD
JIM DAVIS 10·5

GARFIELD...
www.garfield.com
Distributed by Universal Press Syndicate
HOW'S THE DIET GOING?
GREAT!
JIM DAVIS 10·6
YOU HAVE FROSTING ON YOUR LIPS
I PILLAGED A BAKE SALE
© 2001 PAWS, INC. All Rights Reserved.

GARFIELD®
A CANDY BAR! ...BUT I'M ON A DIET...
Distributed by Universal Press Syndicate
www.garfield.com
THIS MUST BE A TEST...
© 2001 PAWS, INC. All Rights Reserved.
-OR A TRICK...
TEST...TRICK...TEST...TRICK...
GRAB
SQUEEK!
AH-HA!
BOTH
JIM DAVIS 10·7

WELL, ONE GOOD THING ABOUT THIS DIET...
JPM DAVPS 10-8
Distributed by Universal Press Syndicate www.garfield.com
-AT LEAST I HAVEN'T HAD ANY OF THOSE WEIRD...
HEY, PAL, HOW'S ABOUT A SNACK?
HALLUCINATIONS
© 2001 PAWS, INC. All Rights Reserved.

SAAAY... **YOU'RE** LOOKING HUNGRY
YOU'RE JUST A DIETARY HALLUCINATION. GO AWAY
Distributed by Universal Press Syndicate www.garfield.com
I CAN'T, UNTIL YOU STOP OBSESSING ABOUT ME
© 2001 PAWS, INC. All Rights Reserved.
JPM DAVPS 10-9
I'D LIKE YOU TO MEET A CLOSE, DEAR AND PERSONAL OBSESSION OF MINE

I'M A DONUT... EAT ME!
NO YOU'RE NOT. YOU'RE JUST A DIET-INDUCED HALLUCINATION
Distributed by Universal Press Syndicate www.garfield.com
NOW I'M FROSTED!
SORRY. YOU'RE NOT REAL
JPM DAVPS 10-10
WITH SPRINKLES!
ALL RIGHT. COME HERE
© 2001 PAWS, INC. All Rights Reserved.

THERE HAS **GOT** TO BE AN EASIER WAY TO LOSE WEIGHT
Distributed by Universal Press Syndicate www.garfield.com
YOU COULD EXERCISE
© 2001 PAWS, INC. All Rights Reserved.
MUNCH MUNCH MUNCH MUNCH MUNCH
NUMMM
JIM DAVIS 10-11

I DON'T THINK I CAN EAT ALL OF MY LETTUCE LEAF
Distributed by Universal Press Syndicate www.garfield.com
© 2001 PAWS, INC. All Rights Reserved.
BECAUSE I'M PLANNING TO PASS OUT FROM HUNGER!
JIM DAVIS 10-12

CELERY!
Distributed by Universal Press Syndicate www.garfield.com
IF SCIENCE COULD FIND A USE FOR IT, WE WOULDN'T HAVE TO EAT IT TO GET RID OF IT!
© 2001 PAWS, INC. All Rights Reserved.
DIET STARTING TO GET TO YOU?
JIM DAVIS 10-13

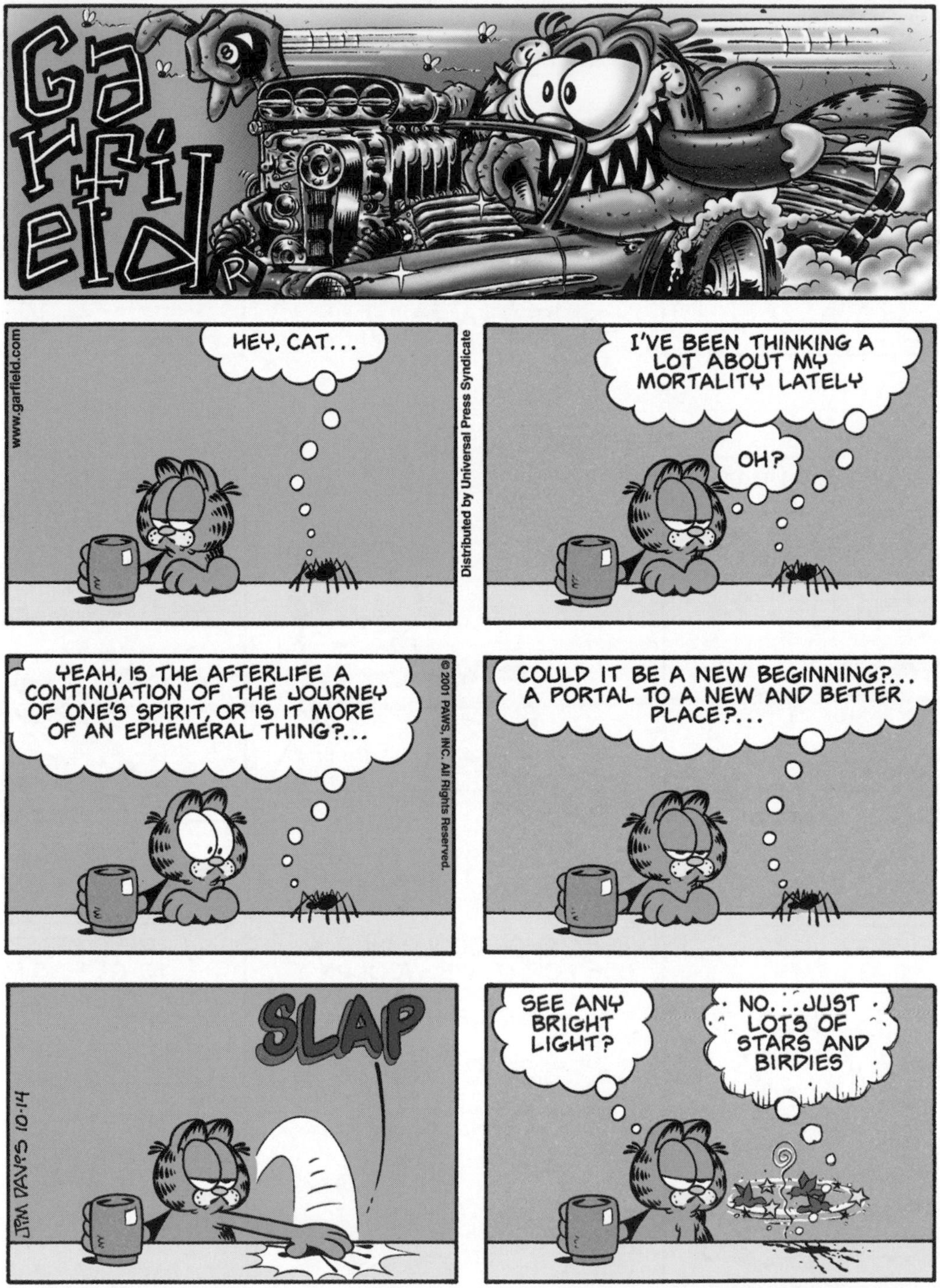
GARFIELD
www.garfield.com
Distributed by Universal Press Syndicate
HEY, CAT...
I'VE BEEN THINKING A LOT ABOUT MY MORTALITY LATELY
OH?
© 2001 PAWS, INC. All Rights Reserved.
YEAH, IS THE AFTERLIFE A CONTINUATION OF THE JOURNEY OF ONE'S SPIRIT, OR IS IT MORE OF AN EPHEMERAL THING?...
COULD IT BE A NEW BEGINNING?... A PORTAL TO A NEW AND BETTER PLACE?...
SLAP
JIM DAVIS 10·14
SEE ANY BRIGHT LIGHT?
NO...JUST LOTS OF STARS AND BIRDIES

IF YOU FINISH YOUR CARROT, YOU MAY HAVE ANOTHER
JIM DAVIS 10-15
Distributed by Universal Press Syndicate www.garfield.com
© 2001 PAWS, INC. All Rights Reserved.
FINISHED

THAT WAS THE VET. SHE SAYS YOU CAN GO OFF YOUR DIET NOW
JIM DAVIS 10-16
Distributed by Universal Press Syndicate www.garfield.com
THUD
© 2001 PAWS, INC. All Rights Reserved.
ARE YOU ALL RIGHT?!
QUICK! MOUTH-TO-MEAT LOAF RESUSCITATION!

YOU'RE BEING ANNOYING, ODIE
Distributed by Universal Press Syndicate www.garfield.com
STILL ANNOYING
© 2001 PAWS, INC. All Rights Reserved.
NOT QUITE GETTING THE DRIFT, ARE YOU, PAL?
JIM DAVIS 10-17

YOUR POINTY ELBOWS GIVE ME A HEADACHE
JIM DAVIS 10-18
www.garfield.com
Distributed by Universal Press Syndicate
YOU LOST ME THERE, JON...
© 2001 PAWS, INC. All Rights Reserved.
THAT MAKES NO SENSE AT ALL

WHY AM I ALWAYS HAVING TO BEG FOR DATES?! I'M GOING TO LET THE GIRLS CALL ME!
JIM DAVIS 10-19
www.garfield.com
Distributed by Universal Press Syndicate
© 2001 PAWS, INC. All Rights Reserved.
DR. LIVINGSTONE, I PRESUME?

GARFIELD, THE KID ACROSS THE STREET HAS LOST HIS TURTLE
JIM DAVIS 10-20
www.garfield.com
Distributed by Universal Press Syndicate
YOU DON'T SAY
© 2001 PAWS, INC. All Rights Reserved.
CAN HE DESCRIBE IT?

GARFIELD®
BURRRRRRRP
BUURRRRRRAAP
BUUURRUUP
BRAAAAP
BURP
NICE TRY... MERE MORTAL
JIM DAVIS 10·21

JIM DAVIS 10·22
Distributed by Universal Press Syndicate www.garfield.com
WHOOOOMP!
© 2001 PAWS, INC. All Rights Reserved.
BUNGEE DOGGGG!

JIM DAVIS 10·23
Distributed by Universal Press Syndicate www.garfield.com
TOING!
?
© 2001 PAWS, INC. All Rights Reserved.
SLING-SHOT DOOOGGG!!

SHIKKA SHIKKA SHIKKA
SHIKKA SHIKKA SHIKKA
JIM DAVIS 10·24
Distributed by Universal Press Syndicate www.garfield.com
© 2001 PAWS, INC. All Rights Reserved.
AAATTIC DOOOGGG!!

© 2001 PAWS, INC. All Rights Reserved.
Distributed by Universal Press Syndicate
www.garfield.com
JIM DAVIS 10·25
ROOOOF DOOOGGG!!

EEEWW... COLD COFFEE
JIM DAVIS 10·26
www.garfield.com
Distributed by Universal Press Syndicate
WHOOMPO
© 2001 PAWS, INC. All Rights Reserved.
WARM-UP DOOOGGG!

DING-DONG
www.garfield.com
Distributed by Universal Press Syndicate
DING-DONG
DOOORRRR DOOOGGG!
© 2001 PAWS, INC. All Rights Reserved.
JIM DAVIS 10·27

Garfield
www.garfield.com
Distributed by Universal Press Syndicate
SIGH
I HAVE NO LIFE...
JON HAS NO LIFE...
ODIE HAS...
SLURRP
SLURP SLURP SLURP
SLURP SLURP SLURP
VEEEEEERY LITTLE LIFE LEFT
JPM DAVIS 10-28
© 2001 PAWS, INC. All Rights Reserved.

A COOKIE CHOCOLATE CHIP
JIM DAVIS 10-29
Distributed by Universal Press Syndicate www.garfield.com
© 2001 PAWS, INC. All Rights Reserved.

GOOD DOG
JIM DAVIS 10-30
Distributed by Universal Press Syndicate www.garfield.com
BAD DOG
© 2001 PAWS, INC. All Rights Reserved.
COMPLEX, AREN'T THEY?

DOES THE WORD "GLUTTON" MEAN ANYTHING TO YOU?
Distributed by Universal Press Syndicate www.garfield.com
HOW ABOUT "HOG BOY"?
JIM DAVIS 10-31
© 2001 PAWS, INC. All Rights Reserved.
HOW ABOUT "MISTER FATTY-FAT-FAT"?!!
PEOPLE WITHOUT DONUTS ARE SO BITTER

SOME PEOPLE THINK OF PETS AS THEIR CHILDREN
www.garfield.com
Distributed by Universal Press Syndicate
© 2001 PAWS, INC. All Rights Reserved.
SO...DAD. DO YOU HAVE A WILL?
JIM DAVIS 11-1

I HAVE A DATE WITH CINDY, GARFIELD
JIM DAVIS 11-2
www.garfield.com
Distributed by Universal Press Syndicate
SHE LIKES THE STRONG, SILENT TYPE
© 2001 PAWS, INC. All Rights Reserved.
SO I'M DRESSED AS A MUSCLE-BOUND MIME
TRY NOT TO GET BEAT UP

HAVEN'T WE MET SOMEWHERE BEFORE?
JIM DAVIS 11-3
www.garfield.com
Distributed by Universal Press Syndicate
YES
© 2001 PAWS, INC. All Rights Reserved.
I WONDER IF THAT'S GOOD OR BAD
SHE'S PICKING UP A ROCK!

Garfield®
AHHH...THERE SHE IS
A LITTLE TO THE LEFT...
A LITTLE MORE... THAT'S IT...
A LIIIIIIITLE MORE...
WOOOOOOH!
SNAP
THUD
WHO DUG THE TIGER TRAP IN MRS. FEENY'S FLOWER BED?!
WEEEEEEE
I LOVE SIRENS!
JIM DAVIS 11-4

Distributed by Universal Press Syndicate www.garfield.com
© 2001 PAWS, INC. All Rights Reserved.
OH, GARFIELD, MAY I HAVE A WORD WITH YOU?
CAN IT WAIT? I'M BUSY CHASING THE MOUSE
JIM DAVIS 11-5

JIM DAVIS 11-6
Distributed by Universal Press Syndicate www.garfield.com
© 2001 PAWS, INC. All Rights Reserved.
AND DON'T COME BACK!
TOO LATE

CHING CHING
Distributed by Universal Press Syndicate www.garfield.com
CHING CHING
© 2001 PAWS, INC. All Rights Reserved.
WE SEEM TO BE INFESTED WITH COWBOYS
JIM DAVIS 11-7

NOK NOK
JIM DAVIS 11-8
MAY I BORROW A CUP OF SUGAR?
SURE
I SAID A CUP, NOT A THIMBLE!
I CAN'T WIN HERE
COOK BOOK
Distributed by Universal Press Syndicate www.garfield.com
© 2001 PAWS, INC. All Rights Reserved.

GARFIELD!
PRESENT
JIM DAVIS 11-9
WHAT?
HE DIDN'T SEEM VERY HAPPY
THE MAN IS AN ENIGMA
Distributed by Universal Press Syndicate www.garfield.com
© 2001 PAWS, INC. All Rights Reserved.

THE MICE AND I HAVE AN AGREEMENT
I DON'T EAT THEM...
AND THEY DON'T BOOBY TRAP THE LITTER BOX
JIM DAVIS 11-10
Distributed by Universal Press Syndicate www.garfield.com
© 2001 PAWS, INC. All Rights Reserved.

Garfield®
www.garfield.com
IT IS FREEZING IN HERE!
AH-HA! I KNEW I STILL HAD THOSE OLD RUBBER ARMS!
© 2001 PAWS, INC. All Rights Reserved.
Distributed by Universal Press Syndicate
GET AWAY FROM THAT THERMOSTAT!
JIM DAVIS 11-11

DINNER'S RUNNING LATE
www.garfield.com
Distributed by Universal Press Syndicate
FINE
© 2001 PAWS, INC. All Rights Reserved.
ANY LAST WORDS?
JIM DAVIS 11-12

YOU WOULDN'T BE SO HAPPY IF YOU WERE SEEING WHAT I'M SEEING
JIM DAVIS 11-13
www.garfield.com
Distributed by Universal Press Syndicate
ZIP
© 2001 PAWS, INC. All Rights Reserved.
HOW LONG HAVE YOU BEEN CARRYING THAT AROUND WAITING FOR ME TO SAY THAT?!

OW!!!
© 2001 PAWS, INC. All Rights Reserved.
JIM DAVIS 11-14
GARFIELD, YOU OAF! THAT WAS MY FOOT YOU STEPPED ON!
www.garfield.com
Distributed by Universal Press Syndicate
GAAAHH
NOW YOU HAVE A MATCHED SET

WHY YES, JUDY, I AM AS MASCULINE AS I SOUND
JIM DAVIS 11-15
© 2001 PAWS, INC. All Rights Reserved.
O.K. JUDY, YOU'RE ON!
www.garfield.com
Distributed by Universal Press Syndicate
I JUST BOUGHT THREE THOUSAND DOLLARS WORTH OF WINDOWS
WAS JUDY AS SLICK AS SHE SOUNDED?

DING DONG
THAT'S MY DATE. NOW BE NICE
© 2001 PAWS, INC. All Rights Reserved.
EEEEEEK!
www.garfield.com
Distributed by Universal Press Syndicate
I HAVEN'T EVEN OPENED THE **DOOR** YET!
JUST GETTING IT OUT OF THE WAY
JIM DAVIS 11-16

www.garfield.com
Distributed by Universal Press Syndicate
WOW...
© 2001 PAWS, INC. All Rights Reserved.
JIM DAVIS 11-17
TWO BEAUTIFUL DAYS IN A ROW!
I HATE RERUNS

Garfield®
Distributed by Universal Press Syndicate
© 2001 PAWS, INC. All Rights Reserved.
www.garfield.com
JIM DAVIS 11-18
IF YOU THINK YOU'RE PSYCHING ME OUT, YOU'RE MISTAKEN

I'M A BUG
I EAT BUGS
I EAT BIRDS
JIM DAVIS 11-19
www.garfield.com
Distributed by Universal Press Syndicate
MY HERO!
© 2001 PAWS, INC. All Rights Reserved.
STOMP!

BEWARE OF THE DOG
JIM DAVIS 11-20
www.garfield.com
Distributed by Universal Press Syndicate
MONDAY, WEDNESDAY AND FRIDAY
© 2001 PAWS, INC. All Rights Reserved.
IT'S TUESDAY
PENCIL ME IN FOR TOMORROW

JIM DAVIS 11-21
www.garfield.com
Distributed by Universal Press Syndicate
HEY!
© 2001 PAWS, INC. All Rights Reserved.
I WENT TO HIGH SCHOOL WITH THAT SWEATER!

SO, DID YOU FINALLY GET ENOUGH TO EAT?
JIM DAVIS 11-22
www.garfield.com
Distributed by Universal Press Syndicate
DEPENDS...
© 2001 PAWS, INC. All Rights Reserved.
IS THERE ANYTHING LEFT?

SO WHY WON'T YOU GO OUT WITH ME?
JIM DAVIS 11-23
www.garfield.com
Distributed by Universal Press Syndicate
WHAT?! NOT MANLY ENOUGH?!
© 2001 PAWS, INC. All Rights Reserved.
BOY, THAT'LL TAKE THE STARCH OUT OF YOUR PETTICOAT
EASY, BIG FELLA

WHAT DO YOU THINK OF MY NEW SUIT?
YAAAHHH!
www.garfield.com
Distributed by Universal Press Syndicate
MY EYES! MY EYES!
© 2001 PAWS, INC. All Rights Reserved.
AND DON'T SUGARCOAT IT
JIM DAVIS 11-24

Garfield®
www.garfield.com
Distributed by Universal Press Syndicate
© 2001 PAWS, INC. All Rights Reserved.
PAT PAT PAT
NOPE
RATS!
THE HECK WITH IT
I THOUGHT YOU WERE NAPPING
COULDN'T FIND MY SPOT
JIM DAVIS 11-25

I WONDER IF I SHOULD GO FOR A WALK...
Distributed by Universal Press Syndicate www.garfield.com
NO WAY!
I REFUSE!
© 2001 PAWS, INC. All Rights Reserved.
I'M OUTVOTED
JIM DAVIS 11-26

WHENEVER THINGS ARE MISSING THEY CALL ON A DOG TO TRACK IT DOWN
Distributed by Universal Press Syndicate www.garfield.com
© 2001 PAWS, INC. All Rights Reserved.
HAS IT OCCURRED TO ANYONE THAT DOGS MIGHT BE TAKING THAT STUFF TO BEGIN WITH?
JIM DAVIS 11-27

THE WORLD IS CONSTANTLY CHANGING
Distributed by Universal Press Syndicate www.garfield.com
© 2001 PAWS, INC. All Rights Reserved.
THEY HAVEN'T STOPPED MAKING FROZEN PUDDING POPS, HAVE THEY?
JIM DAVIS 11-28

BEWARE OF THE Artistic DOG
SCRIBBLE SCRIBBLE SCRIBBLE
ZIP
MY NOSE ISN'T THAT BIG!
JIM DAVIS 11-29
Distributed by Universal Press Syndicate www.garfield.com
© 2001 PAWS, INC. All Rights Reserved.

GARFIELD, I'M GOING TO ASK THE FIRST WOMAN I SEE TO GO OUT
JIM DAVIS 11-30
THE FIRST ONE WITHOUT A MONKEY
SHE LOOKED INTERESTING
Distributed by Universal Press Syndicate www.garfield.com
© 2001 PAWS, INC. All Rights Reserved.

I'M SPENDING THE EVENING WITH A CAT!
HA! HA! HA!
HEY!
JIM DAVIS 12-1
Distributed by Universal Press Syndicate www.garfield.com
© 2001 PAWS, INC. All Rights Reserved.

GARFIELD
TAP
TAP
TAP
www.garfield.com
SLAM!
Distributed by Universal Press Syndicate
VRRRMMMM
R-R-R-R-R-R-R
© 2001 PAWS, INC. All Rights Reserved.
JIM DAVIS 12-2
I TOLD YOU, I AM **NOT** GOING CHRISTMAS SHOPPING TODAY!
BUT THE CAR'S ALL WARMED UP!

BOYS! HOT CHOCOLATE!
www.garfield.com
Distributed by Universal Press Syndicate
ZIP ZIP
© 2001 PAWS, INC. All Rights Reserved.
WHERE'S ODIE?
I'M STANDING ON HIM
JIM DAVIS 12-3

SANTA IS COMING SOON. HAVE YOU BEEN GOOD THIS YEAR?
www.garfield.com
Distributed by Universal Press Syndicate
JIM DAVIS 12-4
© 2001 PAWS, INC. All Rights Reserved.
YES, I HAVE
TOO LATE! I SAW YOUR PUPILS DILATE!

NO, NO, NO!!!
www.garfield.com
Distributed by Universal Press Syndicate
IT'S SIX EYELASHES ON EACH DOLL... SIX! GET IT RIGHT!
JIM DAVIS 12-5
© 2001 PAWS, INC. All Rights Reserved.
WE WILL RETURN TO "STEWEY, THE ANAL-RETENTIVE ELF"...
MAYBE YOU WILL...

"Dear Jonathan Q. Arbuckle,"
"a very Happy Holidays to you, Jonathan Q. Arbuckle, and yours on this, the most joyous time of year, Jonathan Q. Arbuckle."
JIM DAVIS 12-6
© 2001 PAWS, INC. All Rights Reserved.
Distributed by Universal Press Syndicate
HOW SWEET
HE LOVES THE FOLKS AT THE INSURANCE COMPANY

JIM DAVIS 12-7
HAVE YOU WRITTEN YOUR LETTER TO SANTA YET?
RIIINNG
Distributed by Universal Press Syndicate
www.garfield.com
HELLO?
THIS IS SANTA
© 2001 PAWS, INC. All Rights Reserved.
...YOU PAGED MY BEEPER?
HERE'S MY LIST

Distributed by Universal Press Syndicate
www.garfield.com
SLUURRP!
AAAGGHH
© 2001 PAWS, INC. All Rights Reserved.
JIM DAVIS 12-8
EWW...WHAT IS HE DOING?
WRINGING OUT HIS BEARD
VISIT SANTA

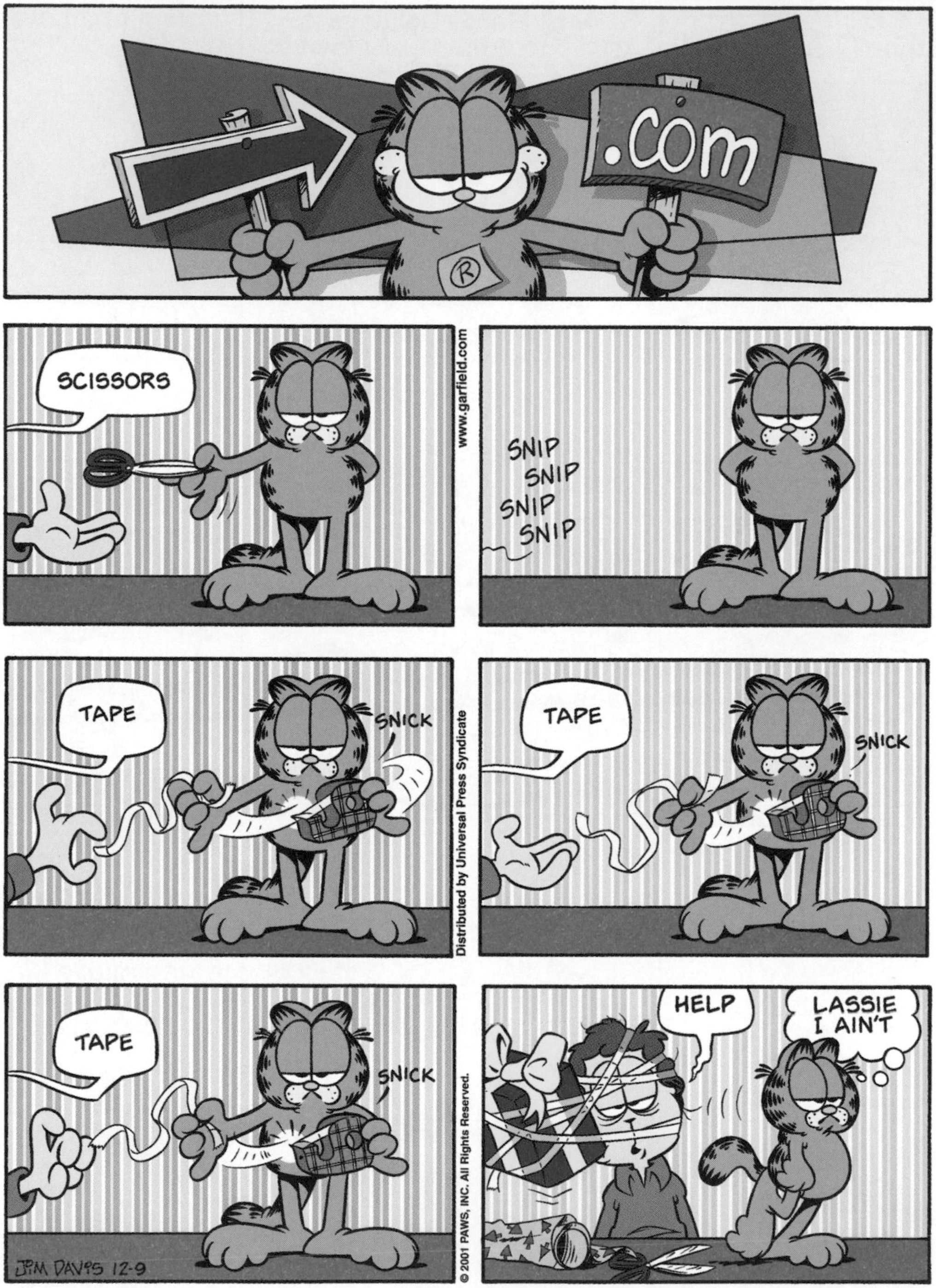
.com
SCISSORS
www.garfield.com
SNIP
SNIP
SNIP
SNIP
TAPE
SNICK
Distributed by Universal Press Syndicate
TAPE
SNICK
TAPE
SNICK
JPM DAVPS 12-9
© 2001 PAWS, INC. All Rights Reserved.
HELP
LASSIE I AIN'T

JIM DAVIS 12-10
I'M FEELING ALL CHRISTMASY!
www.garfield.com
Distributed by Universal Press Syndicate
I KNOW...
© 2001 PAWS, INC. All Rights Reserved.
IT'S CATCHING!

SO DID YOU PUT UP A TREE AND EVERYTHING?
OH, YEAH
Distributed by Universal Press Syndicate
www.garfield.com
ONLY THIS YEAR WE WENT WITH AN ARTIFICIAL ONE
ARTIFICIAL?
JIM DAVIS 12-11
© 2001 PAWS, INC. All Rights Reserved.
YEAH, IT'S ONE OF THOSE PINE-SCENTED AIR FRESHENERS SHAPED LIKE A DOUGLAS FIR

GUESS WHAT, ELLEN... I HAVE MISTLETOE!
JIM DAVIS 12-12
www.garfield.com
Distributed by Universal Press Syndicate
IF I HOLD IT OVER YOUR HEAD, YOU HAVE TO KISS ME
© 2001 PAWS, INC. All Rights Reserved.
YEAH, WELL IT'S THE LAW, ELLEN!
THERE ARE WORSE THINGS THAN JAIL

WE NOW RETURN TO "EDWARD FERNBERGLE, THE CERTIFIED PUBLIC ACCOUNTANT WHO SAVED CHRISTMAS"
JIM DAVIS 12-13
© 2001 PAWS, INC. All Rights Reserved.
RIIING RIIING
HELLO?
Distributed by Universal Press Syndicate
www.garfield.com
SANTA, THE ELVES HAVE BEEN SKIMMING FROM PETTY CASH!
ED! YOU'VE SAVED US!
SLAP THEM IN TINY IRONS!

HI, MOM? IT'S JON
© 2001 PAWS, INC. All Rights Reserved.
www.garfield.com
Distributed by Universal Press Syndicate
I'M CALLING BECAUSE I NEED YOUR TOP-SECRET RECIPE FOR CHRISTMAS COOKIES!
JIM DAVIS 12-14
NO, MOM, THE LINE IS NOT TAPPED
ARE YOU SURE?

BEFORE TOO LONG IT'LL BE TIME TO GET A NEW CHRISTMAS TREE
© 2001 PAWS, INC. All Rights Reserved.
SO I GUESS WE OUGHT TO TAKE THE OLD ONE DOWN
CAN'T WE JUST SCOOT IT OVER...
Distributed by Universal Press Syndicate
www.garfield.com
NEXT TO THE OTHER ONE?
JIM DAVIS
12-15

GARFIELD
JUST CALLED TO WISH YOU HAPPY HOLIDAYS, MOM! WHA?...YES, I ATE JUST A FEW HOURS AGO...HMM? WHO? SURE! PUT HIM ON!
www.garfield.com
HI'YA, DAD! HAPPY HOLIDAYS!...I'M FINE...YEP, CHANGED MY OIL LAST WEEK...GRANDMA? SURE! PUT HER ON!
HI, GRANDMA!...I SAID HI!!...NOPE ...STILL SINGLE...SINGLE!! ...SINGLE!!!
© 2001 PAWS, INC. All Rights Reserved.
DOC BOY?... DOC BOY?! SURE...PUT HIM ON!!!
HELLO? HELLO?
JIM DAVIS 12-16
Distributed by Universal Press Syndicate
TALK INTO THE OTHER END, DOC BOY!
HAPPY HOLIDAYS, ALL YOU FAMILY MEMBERS OUT THERE

I'M LOOKING FOR A CHRISTMAS TREE
WHO ISN'T?
A GREAT BIG ONE!
I LIKE YOUR STYLE
LET'S TALK **HUGE!**
LET'S TALK FINANCING
JIM DAVIS 12-17
www.garfield.com
Distributed by Universal Press Syndicate
© 2001 PAWS, INC. All Rights Reserved.

I CAN'T BELIEVE WHAT YOU CHARGE FOR A CHRISTMAS TREE!
JIM DAVIS 12-18
© 2001 PAWS, INC. All Rights Reserved.
WELL, WE DO ALSO SELL THE KIT...
KIT?
THIS IS A **PINE CONE!**
SOME ASSEMBLY REQUIRED
Distributed by Universal Press Syndicate
www.garfield.com

I'M GOING OUT TO HANG THE CHRISTMAS LIGHTS ON THE HOUSE
JIM DAVIS 12-19
© 2001 PAWS, INC. All Rights Reserved.
REMEMBER NOW...
I KNOW, I KNOW...
www.garfield.com
Distributed by Universal Press Syndicate
IF I HEAR A SCREAM, CALL THE FIRE DEPARTMENT. FOR A SCREAM AND A "BZZZT," CALL THE POWER COMPANY. FOR A SCREAM, A "BZZZT" AND A "THUD," CALL AN AMBULANCE

SHAKE SHAKE SHAKE
AHEM
© 2001 PAWS, INC. All Rights Reserved.
YOU'RE NOT PEEKING, ARE YOU?
GARFIELD
www.garfield.com
Distributed by Universal Press Syndicate
ONLY WITH MY EARS
JIM DAVIS 12-20

JIM DAVIS 12-21
© 2001 PAWS, INC. All Rights Reserved.
SNIFFFFFFFF
Distributed by Universal Press Syndicate
www.garfield.com
YOU'RE LOOKING CHEERFUL THIS MORNING
I JUST TANKED UP ON CHRISTMAS SPIRIT

HI, CAT
HI, FLEA
© 2001 PAWS, INC. All Rights Reserved.
JUST WANTED TO STOP BY AND SAY MERRY CHRISTMAS BEFORE I TAKE OFF
WHERE TO?
www.garfield.com
Distributed by Universal Press Syndicate
OH, I'M CATCHING A GREYHOUND TO KANSAS CITY
JIM DAVIS 12-22

Garfield
www.garfield.com
Distributed by Universal Press Syndicate
POP
© 2001 PAWS, INC. All Rights Reserved.
JIM DAVIS 12-23
MERRY CHRISTMAS

CHRISTMAS EVE, AND I CAN'T SLEEP
I NEED A SEDATIVE
QUICK, TELL ME A STORY ABOUT YOUR BOYHOOD ON THE FARM
JIM DAVIS 12·24
www.garfield.com Distributed by Universal Press Syndicate
© 2001 PAWS, INC. All Rights Reserved.

HEY!
JIM DAVIS 12·25
YOU KNOW, THAT SANTA IS EVEN NICER THAN I THOUGHT...
HE LEFT ME A COOKIE!
FOR GARFIELD
SANTA
MERRY CHRISTMAS!
www.garfield.com Distributed by Universal Press Syndicate
© 2001 PAWS, INC. All Rights Reserved.

HI, MOM?... IT'S JON
JIM DAVIS 12·26
ABOUT THAT SWEATER YOU MADE GARFIELD FOR CHRISTMAS?...
YOU LEFT OUT A HOLE
HOW DO YOU LEAVE OUT A HOLE?!
www.garfield.com Distributed by Universal Press Syndicate
© 2001 PAWS, INC. All Rights Reserved.

KAREN, HOW'D YOU LIKE TO GO OUT WITH ME ON NEW YEAR'S EVE?
WHAT'S IT WORTH TO YOU?
UH... PAINT YOUR HOUSE?
I LIKE THIS ONE ALREADY
JIM DAVIS 12-27
www.garfield.com
Distributed by Universal Press Syndicate
© 2001 PAWS, INC. All Rights Reserved.

NONE OF THE GIRLS I CALLED WANT TO GO OUT WITH ME ON NEW YEAR'S EVE
MAYBE IF I CALLED THEM AGAIN AND USED A FRENCH ACCENT...
WHO NEEDS CABLE TV WHEN YOU'VE GOT THIS?
JIM DAVIS 12-28
© 2001 PAWS, INC. All Rights Reserved.
www.garfield.com
Distributed by Universal Press Syndicate

CAN YOU BELIEVE IT?! PATTI BROKE OUR DATE, AND NOW I'M STUCK WITH TWO TICKETS TO THE NEW YEAR'S EVE DANCE!
NOW WHAT DO I DO?
DUH...
GO STAG, SCALP THE OTHER TICKET AT THE DOOR, AND BUY ME SOMETHING
JIM DAVIS 12-29
Distributed by Universal Press Syndicate
www.garfield.com
© 2001 PAWS, INC. All Rights Reserved.

# Outrageous Outtakes Part Deux

THIS BOOK IS DONE...
ON TO MORE FUN!

# Garfield
# OLDER & WIDER

BY JIM DAVIS

**Ballantine Books • New York**

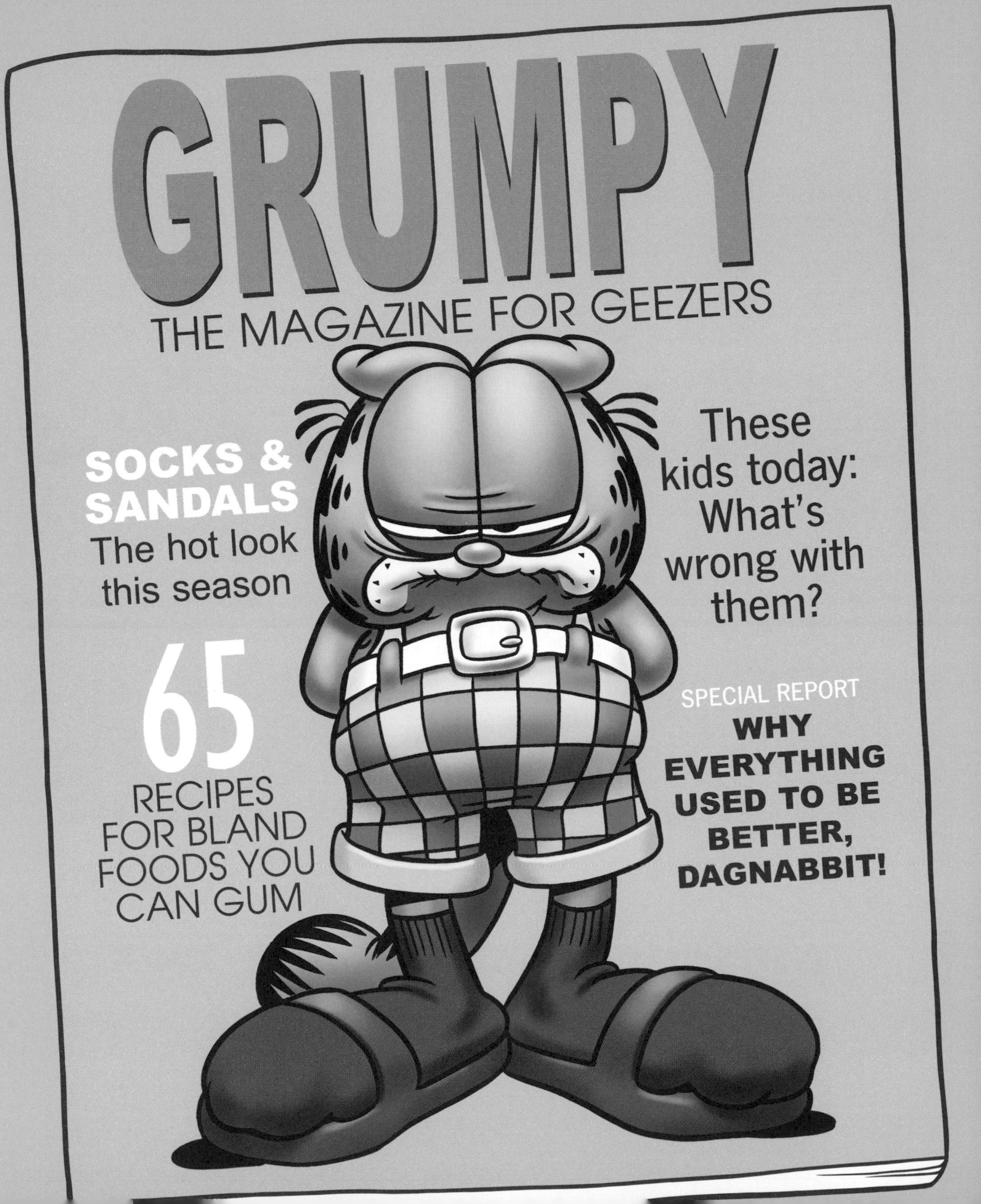
GRUMPY
THE MAGAZINE FOR GEEZERS
SOCKS & SANDALS
The hot look this season
65
RECIPES FOR BLAND FOODS YOU CAN GUM
These kids today: What's wrong with them?
SPECIAL REPORT
WHY EVERYTHING USED TO BE BETTER, DAGNABBIT!

GARFIELD
Distributed by Universal Press Syndicate
© 2001 PAWS, INC. All Rights Reserved.
www.garfield.com
WE NEED A BLOW-DRYER, AND A REALLY, REALLY LONG EXTENSION CORD
JIM DAVIS 12-30

WHY CAN'T I GET A DATE FOR NEW YEAR'S EVE, GARFIELD?
WHY, WHY, WHY, WHY?!
WHY, WHY, WHY, WHY, WHY, WHY, WHY?!!
CAN YOU SAY "MATURE"?
JIM DAVIS 12-31
Distributed by Universal Press Syndicate
www.garfield.com
© 2001 PAWS, INC. All Rights Reserved.

EVERYONE SHOULD DO THEIR BEST
WHICH, HOPEFULLY, WILL ALLOW ME TO GET BY WITHOUT DOING MUCH OF ANYTHING!
JIM DAVIS 1-1
Distributed by Universal Press Syndicate
www.garfield.com
© 2002 PAWS, INC. All Rights Reserved.

I'M NOT GETTING ENOUGH OUT OF LIFE
I MUST EXPEND MORE EFFORT!
Z
Z
JIM DAVIS 1-2
Distributed by Universal Press Syndicate
www.garfield.com
© 2002 PAWS, INC. All Rights Reserved.

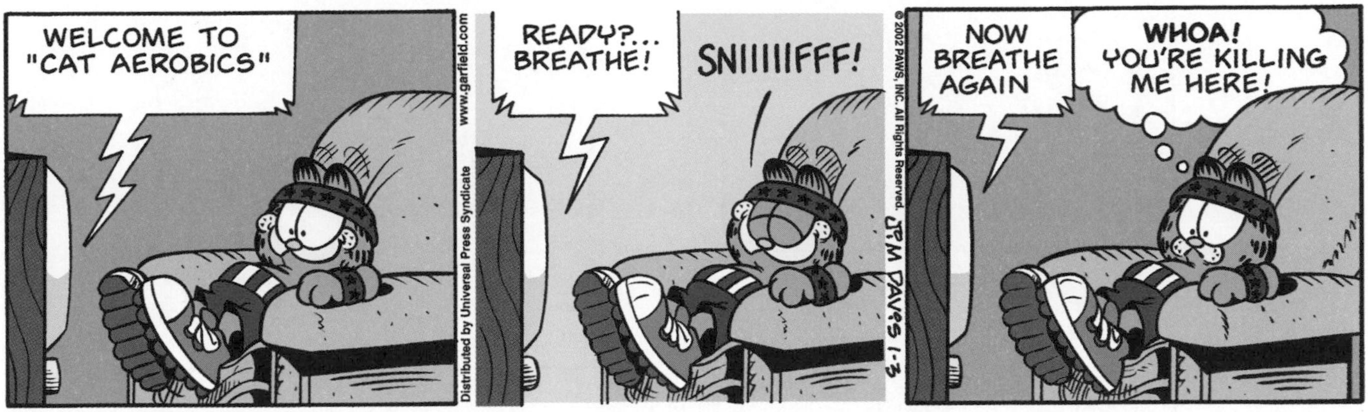
WELCOME TO "CAT AEROBICS"
www.garfield.com
Distributed by Universal Press Syndicate
READY?... BREATHE!
SNIIIIIFFF!
JIM DAVIS 1-3
© 2002 PAWS, INC. All Rights Reserved.
NOW BREATHE AGAIN
WHOA! YOU'RE KILLING ME HERE!

HOW ABOUT A HUG, GARFIELD?
www.garfield.com
Distributed by Universal Press Syndicate
CANDY? BISCUIT? SEAFOOD?
© 2002 PAWS, INC. All Rights Reserved.
NO HUG?
I NEED MOTIVATION
JIM DAVIS 1-4

*BEEP*...YOU HAVE NO MESSAGES
CLICK
JIM DAVIS 1-5
www.garfield.com
Distributed by Universal Press Syndicate
*BEEP* YOU STILL HAVE NO MESSAGES
CLICK
© 2002 PAWS, INC. All Rights Reserved.
HERE'S A MESSAGE FOR YOU... YOU'RE A LOSER!
STOP TORMENTING IT

GARFIELD
CAT HAIR!! THERE IS CAT HAIR EVERYWHERE!!
www.garfield.com
NO! WAIT!
© 2002 PAWS, INC. All Rights Reserved.
HA! YOU MISSED A SPOT!
Distributed by Universal Press Syndicate
FLICK
JIM DAVIS 1-6
I MUST BE SLIPPING
AAAGGGHH!

HAPPY CAT
ANGRY CAT
HAPPY-TO-BE-ANGRY CAT
JIM DAVIS 1-7
Distributed by Universal Press Syndicate www.garfield.com
© 2002 PAWS, INC. All Rights Reserved.

WE'RE HAVING LEFTOVERS FOR DINNER, GARFIELD...
MEAT LOAF...
AND SOMETHING YELLOW
MUSTARD. I'LL TELL MYSELF IT'S MUSTARD
JIM DAVIS 1-8
Distributed by Universal Press Syndicate www.garfield.com
© 2002 PAWS, INC. All Rights Reserved.

I'M GOING TO MAKE A LIST OF THINGS I CAN DO TO IMPRESS WOMEN
"CAN MAKE A LIST..."
HE'S WRITING THAT IN **INK**, LADIES!
JIM DAVIS 1-9
Distributed by Universal Press Syndicate www.garfield.com
© 2002 PAWS, INC. All Rights Reserved.

I'M NOT SAYING JON HAS A BAD WARDROBE
www.garfield.com
Distributed by Universal Press Syndicate
BUT I JUST LOOKED IN HIS CLOSET
© 2002 PAWS, INC. All Rights Reserved.
TWO HUNDRED MOTHS COMMITTED SUICIDE
JIM DAVIS 1-10

I'M DEPRESSED, ELLEN
JIM DAVIS 1-11
www.garfield.com
Distributed by Universal Press Syndicate
I COULD USE A GOOD WORD
© 2002 PAWS, INC. All Rights Reserved.
THAT'S A BAD WORD, ELLEN
DON'T SUGARCOAT IT, ELLEN

YOU'RE BREAKING UP WITH ME?
JIM DAVIS 1-12
www.garfield.com
Distributed by Universal Press Syndicate
BUT WE'VE NEVER DATED
© 2002 PAWS, INC. All Rights Reserved.
YOU DON'T WANT TO TAKE ANY CHANCES?
BETTER SAFE THAN SORRY

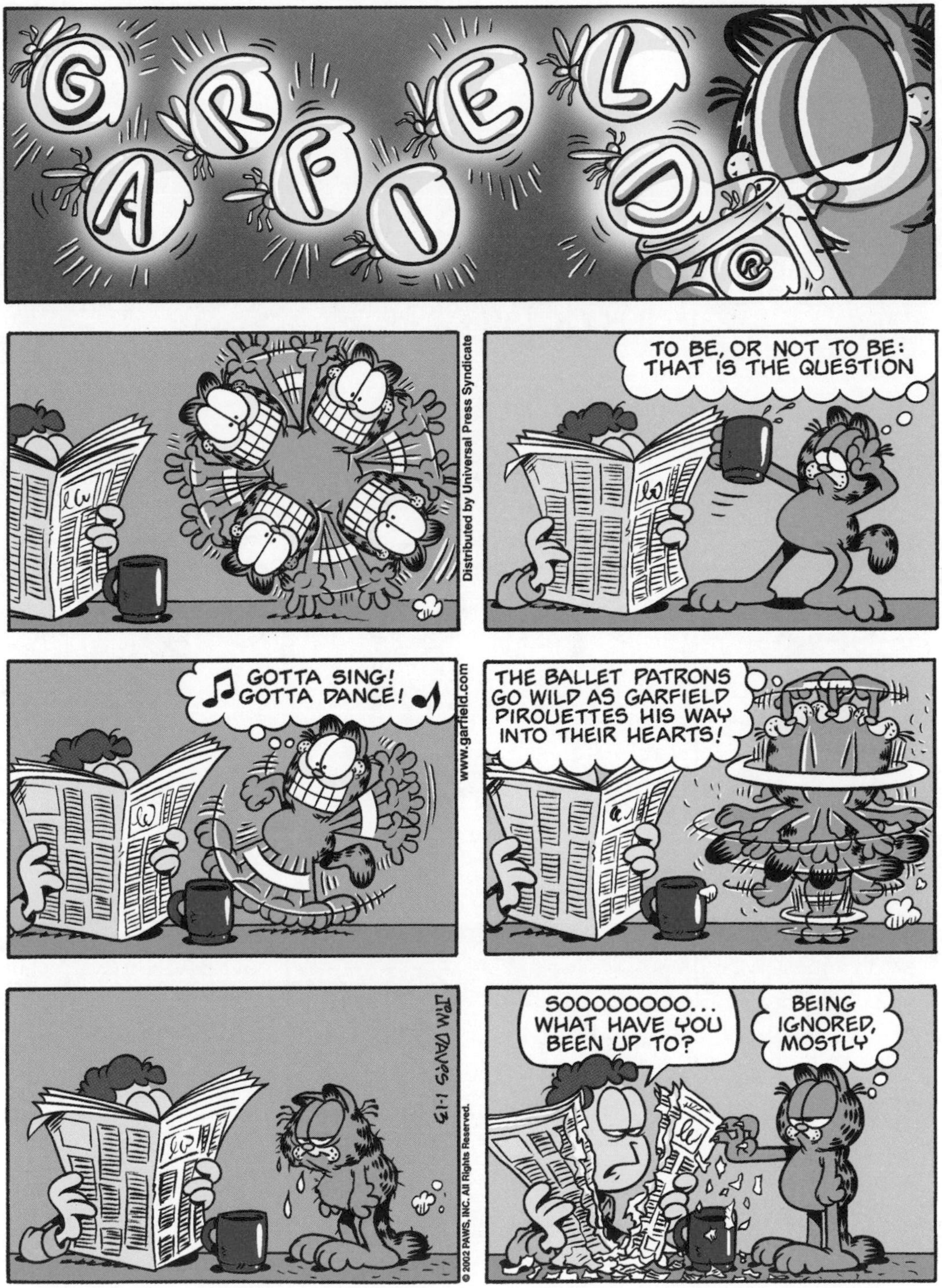
GARFIELD
Distributed by Universal Press Syndicate
TO BE, OR NOT TO BE: THAT IS THE QUESTION
GOTTA SING! GOTTA DANCE!
www.garfield.com
THE BALLET PATRONS GO WILD AS GARFIELD PIROUETTES HIS WAY INTO THEIR HEARTS!
JIM DAVIS 1-13
© 2002 PAWS, INC. All Rights Reserved.
SOOOOOOOO... WHAT HAVE YOU BEEN UP TO?
BEING IGNORED, MOSTLY

GARFIELD, I DON'T THINK YOU COULD GET ANY FATTER
www.garfield.com
Distributed by Universal Press Syndicate
© 2002 PAWS, INC. All Rights Reserved.
THAT WASN'T A CHALLENGE!
I'LL NEED CUPCAKES
JIM DAVIS 1-14

I WENT SHOPPING, GARFIELD
FEED ME
JIM DAVIS 1-15
www.garfield.com
Distributed by Universal Press Syndicate
SPENT EVERY CENT I HAD
FEED ME
© 2002 PAWS, INC. All Rights Reserved.
THESE MOOSE HATS AREN'T CHEAP
SHOOT ME

AND SO ENDS ANOTHER DAY!
JIM DAVIS 1-16
Distributed by Universal Press Syndicate
www.garfield.com
© 2002 PAWS, INC. All Rights Reserved.
WHY DID ODIE GO BACK TO BED?
I'LL BE HAVING HIS BREAKFAST
GARFIELD
ODIE

WHO DESERVES THE LAST DONUT?
JIM DAVIS 1·17
www.garfield.com
Distributed by Universal Press Syndicate
TO BE HONEST...
© 2002 PAWS, INC. All Rights Reserved.
IT PROBABLY WOULD HAVE BEEN YOU

THIS IS REALLY AMAZING, GARFIELD
JIM DAVIS 1·18
Distributed by Universal Press Syndicate
www.garfield.com
I HAVE CALLED EVERY WOMAN I KNOW
© 2002 PAWS, INC. All Rights Reserved.
THEY ALL HAVE A COLD
PROBABLY CAUGHT IT IN GROUP THERAPY

DO YOU HAVE ANY UNFULFILLED DREAMS, GARFIELD?
JIM DAVIS 1·19
www.garfield.com
Distributed by Universal Press Syndicate
OH, SURE
© 2002 PAWS, INC. All Rights Reserved.
THERE'S THE ONE ABOUT THE 12-FOOT CHOCOLATE ÉCLAIR...

GARFIELD®
www.garfield.com
...A WORD WITH YOU?
Distributed by Universal Press Syndicate
THE PET DOOR IS FOR PETS...
AND THE DOOR DOOR IS FOR PEOPLE. NO EXCEPTIONS
YOU KNOW THAT, AND YOU'VE ALWAYS KNOWN THAT
© 2002 PAWS, INC. All Rights Reserved.
SO I'M AFRAID I'M GOING TO HAVE TO ASK YOU TO RETURN YOUR HOUSE KEY
JIM DAVIS 1·20
SORRY ABOUT THAT
IT'S OKAY. I HAD COPIES MADE

HERE'S A JOKE. HOW MANY MICE DOES IT TAKE TO SCREW IN A LIGHTBULB?
MICE DON'T CHANGE LIGHTBULBS. YOU SEE, LIGHTBULBS ARE TOO LARGE AND CUMBERSOME, NOT TO MENTION THAT IT'S MUCH SAFER FOR US TO PILFER FOOD IN THE DARK
THAT JOKE TOOK A SOBERING TURN
JPM DAVIS 1-21
Distributed by Universal Press Syndicate
www.garfield.com
© 2002 PAWS, INC. All Rights Reserved.

JPM DAVIS 1-22
WHAT ARE YOU GOING TO DO ABOUT ALL THESE MICE?
GET THEM NAME TAGS?
Distributed by Universal Press Syndicate
www.garfield.com
© 2002 PAWS, INC. All Rights Reserved.

GARFIELD, HOW DO YOU EXPLAIN THIS?
JPM DAVIS 1-23
HMMM...NEW MOUSE, HIGHER-THAN-AVERAGE DISPOSABLE INCOME, HEAVILY INTO BAROQUE ROCOCO, I'D SAY
Distributed by Universal Press Syndicate
www.garfield.com
© 2002 PAWS, INC. All Rights Reserved.

JIM DAVIS 1-24
www.garfield.com
Distributed by Universal Press Syndicate
I HAVE THE MOUSE CHASING HIMSELF
© 2002 PAWS, INC. All Rights Reserved.
THAT'S CALLED DELEGATING AUTHORITY

THERE GOES A MOUSE!
www.garfield.com
Distributed by Universal Press Syndicate
AREN'T YOU GOING AFTER HIM?!
PERHAPS...
© 2002 PAWS, INC. All Rights Reserved.
THAT IS, IF HE'S GOING TO THE BEACH
JIM DAVIS 1-25

WELL, I HAVE TO GET BACK TO WORK AS A HOUSEHOLD PEST
www.garfield.com
Distributed by Universal Press Syndicate
SIGH
© 2002 PAWS, INC. All Rights Reserved.
ALL THE GOOD JOBS ARE TAKEN
JIM DAVIS 1-26

LICK
LICK
LICK
LICK
LICK
LICK
LICK
LICK
LICK LICK
LICK LICK
LICK
LICK
LI-
DO YOU
MIND?!
JIM DAVIS 1-27
www.garfield.com
Distributed by Universal Press Syndicate
© 2002 PAWS, INC. All Rights Reserved.

WORK HARD AND DO YOUR BEST
www.garfield.com
Distributed by Universal Press Syndicate
© 2002 PAWS, INC. All Rights Reserved.
IT'LL MAKE IT EASIER ON THE REST OF US
JIM DAVIS 1-28

I'M SORRY, MRS. FEENY...
JIM DAVIS 1-29
www.garfield.com
Distributed by Universal Press Syndicate
YES, I'LL LOOK INTO IT
SLAM!
© 2002 PAWS, INC. All Rights Reserved.
IS THAT MRS. FEENY'S WIG?!
IT FOLLOWED ME HOME

NOTHING CAN GO WRONG IF I JUST SIT HERE
JIM DAVIS 1-30
www.garfield.com
Distributed by Universal Press Syndicate
KKKKK!
© 2002 PAWS, INC. All Rights Reserved.
THAT MAN NEVER CEASES TO AMAZE ME

FEAR NOT, JON!
JPM DAVPS 1·31
© 2002 PAWS, INC. All Rights Reserved.
I'VE PUT ODIE TO WORK PROTECTING OUR HOUSE AND VALUABLES!
Distributed by Universal Press Syndicate
www.garfield.com
TAKE ANYTHING BUT THE FOOD

EDNA, I MIGHT BE LATE PICKING YOU UP TONIGHT
JPM DAVPS 2·1
© 2002 PAWS, INC. All Rights Reserved.
WELL, MY HEAD IS STUCK IN A WASTEBASKET
Distributed by Universal Press Syndicate
www.garfield.com
IT'S A LONG ST...SAAAY... MY VOICE SOUNDS DEEPER...
DON'T WAIT UP, EDNA

I'M STARING AT YOU, GARFIELD!
JPM DAVPS 2·2
© 2002 PAWS, INC. All Rights Reserved.
WHAT DO YOU THINK OF THAT?
www.garfield.com
Distributed by Universal Press Syndicate
HEEEY, WHO **WOULDN'T** WANT TO STARE AT ME?

garfield
...THINGS WERE GOING SO WELL...
I WAS CLEAN-SHAVEN, WEARING MY BEST COLOGNE...
© 2002 PAWS, INC. All Rights Reserved.
-HAD MADE A RESERVATION FOR TWO AT A WONDERFUL RESTAURANT...
WE'D ORDERED OUR MEALS...
Distributed by Universal Press Syndicate
I WAS TELLING HER STORIES ABOUT MY BOYHOOD ON THE FARM...
AND THEN SHE NEARLY DROWNED
THIRD ONE THIS MONTH TO FALL ASLEEP IN HER SOUP
www.garfield.com
JIM DAVIS 2-3

YOU ARE MINE, AND MINE ALONE!
JPM DAVPS 2-4
© 2002 PAWS, INC. All Rights Reserved.
I MAINTAIN TOTAL CONTROL OVER YOU!
www.garfield.com
Distributed by Universal Press Syndicate
CHANNEL UP! CHANNEL DOWN!! UP! DOWN! UP!! DOWN!! MUTE! UNMUTE!!
CLICK CLICK CLICK CLICK CLICK CLICK
TWO NEW "AA" BATTERIES ALWAYS GO RIGHT TO HIS HEAD

AND NOW FOR THE FARM REPORT, HERE'S EARL. ...EARL?
Distributed by Universal Press Syndicate
www.garfield.com
DOUG, A PIG JUST BIT ME
A PIG? WHERE DID HE BITE YOU, EARL?
© 2002 PAWS, INC. All Rights Reserved.
JPM DAVPS 2-5
RIGHT IN THE MUDHOLE, DOUG
WHO SAYS THERE'S NOTHING GOOD ON BEFORE SUNRISE?

WELCOME TO "I'M SO SPECIAL!"
© 2002 PAWS, INC. All Rights Reserved.
JPM DAVPS 2-6
...AND WHAT MAKES YOU "SO SPECIAL," SIR?
I CAN WHISTLE THE NATIONAL ANTHEM OUT OF MY LEFT NOSTRIL
Distributed by Universal Press Syndicate
www.garfield.com
AND YOUR RIGHT NOSTRIL?
THAT'S WHERE I UNFURL A TINY FLAG
LET'S HEAR IT FOR PATRIOTISM

TONIGHT, A MAD SCIENTIST PUTS A DOG'S BRAIN INTO A ZOMBIE
JIM DAVIS 2-7
© 2002 PAWS, INC. All Rights Reserved.
IN THE HORROR CLASSIC...
Distributed by Universal Press Syndicate
www.garfield.com
"NIGHT OF THE LIVING DUMB"
WHAT A CRUEL THING TO DO TO A ZOMBIE

TONIGHT, ON "YOU'D BETTER BELIEVE IT!"
JIM DAVIS 2-8
© 2002 PAWS, INC. All Rights Reserved.
...WE VISIT WITH A MAN WHO OWNS A HIPPO!
www.garfield.com
Distributed by Universal Press Syndicate
♪HEEERE, HOLLY! HERE, GIRL!
THAT IS THE BIGGEST PET DOOR I HAVE EVER SEEN!

THE FIRE DEPARTMENT IS HERE...
JIM DAVIS 2-9
© 2002 PAWS, INC. All Rights Reserved.
THE FIRE IS UNDER CONTROL...
www.garfield.com
Distributed by Universal Press Syndicate
AND I'M HAPPY TO REPORT THERE WERE NO INJURIES!
THAT'S THE GOAL OF EVERY COOKING SHOW

GARFIELD
MRS. FEENY REPORTS HER CHIHUAHUA HAS BEEN VARNISHED A DARK CHERRY
Distributed by Universal Press Syndicate
SOMEONE DUCT TAPED ODIE TO OUR SATELLITE DISH...
© 2002 PAWS, INC. All Rights Reserved.
-THERE'S BEEN SO MUCH SHEDDING GOING ON THAT I HACKED UP A HAIRBALL THIS MORNING!
www.garfield.com
AND THE LIVING ROOM DRAPES LOOK LIKE THEY'VE BEEN RUN THROUGH A PAPER SHREDDER!!
I DIDN'T KNOW YOU CARED!
JIM DAVIS 2-10

I'LL NEVER UNDERSTAND YOU
I LIKE THAT...
GARFIELD: CAT OF MYSTERY
JIM DAVIS 2-11
www.garfield.com
Distributed by Universal Press Syndicate
© 2002 PAWS, INC. All Rights Reserved.

LISTEN TO ODIE HOWL LIKE ONE OF HIS WOLF ANCESTORS
EVEN AFTER YEARS OF DOMESTICATION, A DOG IS STILL IN TOUCH WITH PRIMAL URGES A THOUSAND YEARS OLD
LOST HIS INTERNET CONNECTION
JIM DAVIS 2-12
www.garfield.com
Distributed by Universal Press Syndicate
© 2002 PAWS, INC. All Rights Reserved.

AH AH AH
CHOO!
THANK YOU FOR SHARING THAT
AND THANK YOU FOR BEING THERE
JIM DAVIS 2-13
www.garfield.com
Distributed by Universal Press Syndicate
© 2002 PAWS, INC. All Rights Reserved.

SOMETIMES YOU'RE LUCKY
KILLER MOTHS!
AND SOMETIMES YOU'RE JON
JIM DAVIS 2-14
www.garfield.com
Distributed by Universal Press Syndicate
© 2002 PAWS, INC. All Rights Reserved.

READY TO MEET FOR OUR BLIND DATE, EDITH?
HOW WILL I KNOW YOU?
YOU'LL BE CARRYING A SKULL?
STAY IN WELL-LIT AREAS
JIM DAVIS 2-15
www.garfield.com
Distributed by Universal Press Syndicate
© 2002 PAWS, INC. All Rights Reserved.

I HAVE ALL MY TOOLS, GARFIELD
TIME TO TACKLE THOSE HOUSEHOLD PROJECTS
I FEEL LIKE SOMETHING ELECTRICAL...
COULD YOU FIX SOME FOOD UP AHEAD?
JIM DAVIS 2-16
www.garfield.com
Distributed by Universal Press Syndicate
© 2002 PAWS, INC. All Rights Reserved.

garfield®
GOOD NIGHT
www.garfield.com
GOOD NIGHT... GOOD NIGHT...
GOOD NIGHT... GOOD NIGHT...
Distributed by Universal Press Syndicate
-AND GOODBYE
GULP
© 2002 PAWS, INC. All Rights Reserved.
BURRP
MIDNIGHT SNACK
JIM DAVIS 2·17

www.garfield.com
Distributed by Universal Press Syndicate
I'LL BE RIGHT BACK
BLOOT
© 2002 PAWS, INC. All Rights Reserved.
OKAY, WHO PUT THE LEMON WEDGE IN THE FISHBOWL?!

AN EMPTY FISHBOWL...
www.garfield.com
Distributed by Universal Press Syndicate
SIGNS OF A STRUGGLE, AND A CAT WITH A CONTENTED SMILE
© 2002 PAWS, INC. All Rights Reserved.
SOMETHING ISN'T RIGHT HERE
SORRY, CATS, YOU CAN'T HAVE HIM... HE'S TAKEN

WAIT! IF YOU DON'T EAT ME, MAYBE I COULD DO YOU A FAVOR!
www.garfield.com
Distributed by Universal Press Syndicate
WHAT COULD A GOLDFISH EVER DO FOR ME?
© 2002 PAWS, INC. All Rights Reserved.
I KNOW A LOBSTER
I'M LISTENING

GARFIELD, HOW MANY FISH HAVE I OWNED OVER THE YEARS?
www.garfield.com
Distributed by Universal Press Syndicate
THREE HUNDRED TWENTY-ONE?
© 2002 PAWS, INC. All Rights Reserved.
THREE HUNDRED TWENTY-THREE!
OH, YEAH, TWO DIED OF NATURAL CAUSES
JIM DAVIS 2-21

JIM DAVIS 2-22
www.garfield.com
Distributed by Universal Press Syndicate
SCRIBBLE SCRIBBLE SCRIBBLE
© 2002 PAWS, INC. All Rights Reserved.
IS THAT AN I.O.U.?

CONGRATULATIONS, GARFIELD
JIM DAVIS 2-23
www.garfield.com
Distributed by Universal Press Syndicate
YOU'VE EATEN EVERY SINGLE FISH
© 2002 PAWS, INC. All Rights Reserved.
WHAT DO YOU HAVE TO SAY FOR YOURSELF?
DO I GET TO KEEP THE BOWL?

GARFIELD
STOP LOOKING AT ME LIKE THAT...WE ARE NOT LOST
WE'RE JUST A LITTLE OFF TRACK, THAT'S ALL
A FAMILIAR LANDMARK IS ALL I NEED AND I'LL BE FINE...YOU'LL SEE
WE'LL STOP HERE FOR A BITE TO EAT AND THEN BE HOME BEFORE YOU KNOW IT
TWO BURGERS, WITH FRIES
DEES EES DER TOLL BOOT, ZIR
THAT ATTENDANT WAS WEARING LEDERHOSEN
I TOLD YOU TO STOP LOOKING AT ME LIKE THAT
JIM DAVIS 2-24
www.garfield.com
© 2002 PAWS, INC. All Rights Reserved.
Distributed by Universal Press Syndicate

I NEED SOME ATTENTION, GARFIELD
JIM DAVIS 2-25
Distributed by Universal Press Syndicate
www.garfield.com
THAT'LL DO, THANK YOU
GIVE ME A COOKIE AND I'LL GO AWAY
© 2002 PAWS, INC. All Rights Reserved.

ODIE IS PLANNING TO CHASE HIS TAIL
JIM DAVIS 2-26
Distributed by Universal Press Syndicate
www.garfield.com
BUT BEING THE GOOD SPORT HE IS...
HE'S GOING TO GIVE IT A HEAD START
© 2002 PAWS, INC. All Rights Reserved.

SUCCESS ISN'T EVERYTHING IT'S CRACKED UP TO BE
Distributed by Universal Press Syndicate
www.garfield.com
...AND YOU WOULD KNOW THIS BECAAAAUSE?...
© 2002 PAWS, INC. All Rights Reserved.
JIM DAVIS 2-27

SAMMY SOCK PUPPET SAYS HE CAN WHIP YOUR SOCK PUPPET
JIM DAVIS 2-28
www.garfield.com
Distributed by Universal Press Syndicate
YOU TALKIN' 'BOUT BILLY BOOT?
© 2002 PAWS, INC. All Rights Reserved.
NOT FAIR!
AND THE WAR ESCALATES...

ELLEN, I WOULD FORD THE MIGHTIEST RIVER FOR YOU!
www.garfield.com
Distributed by Universal Press Syndicate
WHA?– ...ALL RIGHT
JIM DAVIS 3-1
© 2002 PAWS, INC. All Rights Reserved.
SHE'S CHECKING HER ATLAS FOR PIRANHA-INFESTED TRIBUTARIES
IT PAYS TO DO YOUR HOMEWORK

-AND AFTER I TIED MY SHOE, I TIED THE OTHER ONE...
www.garfield.com
Distributed by Universal Press Syndicate
THEN I THOUGHT ABOUT STANDING UP...
© 2002 PAWS, INC. All Rights Reserved.
JIM DAVIS 3-2
THEN I STOOD UP
IT ACTUALLY TAKES JON LONGER TO TELL ABOUT HIS DAY THAN TO LIVE IT

Garfield®
HERMAN! LONG TIME NO SEE!
WELL, HI, CAT!
Distributed by Universal Press Syndicate
SO, HOW'S THE WIFE AND KIDS?
GREAT, JUST GREAT! YOU'RE LOOKING GOOD...
THANKS! I-
© 2002 PAWS, INC. All Rights Reserved.
JIM DAVIS 3-3
I SUPPOSE I SHOULD CHASE YOU, JUST FOR THE SAKE OF APPEARANCE
NOT TOO FAST, THOUGH...I PULLED A HAMMY ON THE TREADMILL AT THE GYM YESTERDAY
www.garfield.com
YOU'RE BOTH PATHETIC!
RUN FOR YOUR, UH, LIFE, MOUSE
EEK, AND EEK AGAIN. A CAT...

TWO STEAK DINNERS, AND MAKE MINE MEDIUM
AND YOUR BUDDY'S?
MOO
RARE
CHECK
JIM DAVIS 3-4
www.garfield.com Distributed by Universal Press Syndicate
© 2002 PAWS, INC. All Rights Reserved.

HMM...I CAN'T DECIDE BETWEEN THE CHICKEN OR THE FISH...
BUC-BUC BUC-COUGH KAFF-KAFF-KAFF BUC
TRY THE FISH
JIM DAVIS 3-5
www.garfield.com Distributed by Universal Press Syndicate
© 2002 PAWS, INC. All Rights Reserved.

DON'T YOU TWO EVER WANT TO SIT IN A BOOTH?
OH, NO! NEVER!
WHY NOT?
SPIIIIIINNNNN
JIM DAVIS 3-6
Distributed by Universal Press Syndicate www.garfield.com
© 2002 PAWS, INC. All Rights Reserved.

HERE'S YOUR TOSSED SALAD
THANKS
Distributed by Universal Press Syndicate
www.garfield.com
WOULD YOU LIKE FRESH-GROUND PEPPER ON THAT?
JPM DAVIS 3-7
© 2002 PAWS, INC. All Rights Reserved.
HA! HA! HA! HA!
WAH-HA! HA!
DINER HUMOR

WHAT'S THE CATCH OF THE DAY?
PAN-FRIED UGLY FISH
JPM DAVIS 3-8
Distributed by Universal Press Syndicate
www.garfield.com
UHHH...CAN YOU SERVE IT WITHOUT THE HEAD?
NO
© 2002 PAWS, INC. All Rights Reserved.
WHY NOT?
'CAUSE THEN IT WOULDN'T BE **UGLY** NOW, WOULD IT?

HOW ARE YOUR RIBS?
TICKLISH
JPM DAVIS 3-9
www.garfield.com
Distributed by Universal Press Syndicate
I MEANT YOUR BEEF RIBS
© 2002 PAWS, INC. All Rights Reserved.
DON'T KNOW, HON. I'VE NEVER TICKLED A COW
YOU DON'T KNOW WHAT YOU'RE MISSING
I'M NOT WITH THIS MAN

Garfield
www.garfield.com
PECK
PECK
PECK
© 2002 PAWS, INC. All Rights Reserved.
Distributed by Universal Press Syndicate
JIM DAVIS 3-10

SOME DAYS EVERYTHING GOES RIGHT
SMACK!
I MEAN WRONG
JIM DAVIS 3-11
www.garfield.com Distributed by Universal Press Syndicate
© 2002 PAWS, INC. All Rights Reserved.

BURP
YOU DON'T HAVE TO SAVE THOSE FOR ME!
WHAT'S MINE IS YOURS
JIM DAVIS 3-12
Distributed by Universal Press Syndicate www.garfield.com
© 2002 PAWS, INC. All Rights Reserved.

NO MORE, AND THAT'S FINAL!
RFIELD
GARFIELD
SCHLOP!
JIM DAVIS 3-13
Distributed by Universal Press Syndicate
© 2002 PAWS, INC. All Rights Reserved. www.garfield.com

THAT BROWNIE HAS GREEN MOLD GROWING ON IT
www.garfield.com
Distributed by Universal Press Syndicate
© 2002 PAWS, INC. All Rights Reserved.
MAKING IT COUNT AS A VEGETABLE
JIM DAVIS 3-14

ELLEN, I WAS WONDERING...
JIM DAVIS 3-15
www.garfield.com
Distributed by Universal Press Syndicate
WHAT IF WE WERE THE LAST TWO PEOPLE ON EARTH?
© 2002 PAWS, INC. All Rights Reserved.
HUMANITY IS DOOMED
AND CATS WILL RULE THE WORLD!

YOU'VE JUST WON TEN MILLION DOLLARS!
www.garfield.com
Distributed by Universal Press Syndicate
SLAM
JIM DAVIS 3-16
© 2002 PAWS, INC. All Rights Reserved.
WHO WAS IT?
IT WASN'T THE PIZZA GUY

GARFIELD®
HOOOOH!
www.garfield.com
WOOOOOH!
NYAAAH!
Distributed by Universal Press Syndicate
AH-HA
GAAAHHH!
HOT ELASTIC
GHEEEEE!
© 2002 PAWS, INC. All Rights Reserved.
ANNND, HE'S IN THE FRONT YARD
EEEEK!!
SOMEBODY CALL A COP!
JPM DAVPS 3-17

I'M GOING TO MAKE FUN OF DOGS!
MAYBE I'LL GO HOME AND MAKE FUN OF DOGS OVER THE INTERNET
JIM DAVIS 3-18
www.garfield.com
Distributed by Universal Press Syndicate
© 2002 PAWS, INC. All Rights Reserved.

YOU CAN'T CATCH ME!
UH, ARE THOSE NEW RUNNING SHOES?
WHAT HAPPENED TO YOUR TAIL?
IT'S A VICTIM OF NEW INNOVATIONS IN ATHLETIC FOOTWEAR
JIM DAVIS 3-19
www.garfield.com
Distributed by Universal Press Syndicate
© 2002 PAWS, INC. All Rights Reserved.

BEWARE OF THE VICIOUS DOG
...THE REALLY HUGE VIOLENCE-PRONE TEETH-GNASHING DOG
YOU OKAY?
I CAN'T STAND THE PRESSURE!
JIM DAVIS 3-20
www.garfield.com
Distributed by Universal Press Syndicate
© 2002 PAWS, INC. All Rights Reserved.

CHECK OUT THESE SHARP TEETH!
WHOA...
www.garfield.com
Distributed by Universal Press Syndicate
HOW ABOUT THESE CLAWS?
OOO...
JIM DAVIS 3-21
© 2002 PAWS, INC. All Rights Reserved.
WE'VE DECIDED TO GANG UP ON THE MAILMAN

BEWARE OF DOG!
www.garfield.com
Distributed by Universal Press Syndicate
WHO AM I KIDDING? THE THING'S A DISGRACE
© 2002 PAWS, INC. All Rights Reserved.
PLEASE DO NOT KICK THE DOG
THIS IS ALMOST SAD
JIM DAVIS 3-22

BEWARE OF GOPHERS
JIM DAVIS 3-23
Distributed by Universal Press Syndicate
www.garfield.com
BEWARE OF GOPHERS
© 2002 PAWS, INC. All Rights Reserved.
POOK
POOK
POOK

Garfield
www.garfield.com
HEY, TURKEY LEG! WHERE ARE YOU GOING?
I HAVE BEEN A LEFTOVER FOR THREE WEEKS NOW! I KNOW WHEN I'M NOT WANTED!
I'M LEAVING!
TELL ME I DIDN'T SEE THAT
HE'S JUST FEELING UNLOVED. LET'S EAT HIM
JIM DAVIS 3-24
Distributed by Universal Press Syndicate
© 2002 PAWS, INC. All Rights Reserved.

LOOK AT YOU, YOU PIG...
WHY, I BET YOU HAVE MORE FAT THAN MUSCLE
YOU TAKE THAT BACK
JIM DAVIS 3-25
www.garfield.com Distributed by Universal Press Syndicate
© 2002 PAWS, INC. All Rights Reserved.

DON'T BLINK
GARFIELD
TOL' JA
GARFIELD
JIM DAVIS 3-26
Distributed by Universal Press Syndicate www.garfield.com
© 2002 PAWS, INC. All Rights Reserved.

MY HIDDEN CAMERA TOOK THESE PICTURES OF YOU STEALING THE LAST DONUT!
HMM
OKAY, I'D LIKE AN 8×10 OF THIS ONE AND SOME WALLET-SIZED PRINTS OF THESE
JIM DAVIS 3-27
Distributed by Universal Press Syndicate www.garfield.com
© 2002 PAWS, INC. All Rights Reserved.

ODIE
JIM DAVIS 3-28
www.garfield.com
Distributed by Universal Press Syndicate
SPLUT!
ODIE
© 2002 PAWS, INC. All Rights Reserved.
OPEN YOUR MOUTH FIRST!
ODIE
FOOD COACH

WHADDAYA THINK?
YOU'RE WEARING THAT...TO A MONSTER TRUCK RALLY?
www.garfield.com
Distributed by Universal Press Syndicate
TO MEET A BLIND DATE WITH A GOLD TOOTH?
© 2002 PAWS, INC. All Rights Reserved.
JIM DAVIS 3-29

GARFIELD! GET YOUR PAW OUT OF THE COOKIE JAR!
www.garfield.com
Distributed by Universal Press Syndicate
© 2002 PAWS, INC. All Rights Reserved.
WHO TAUGHT YOU THAT GESTURE?!
YOU, IN THE CAR, WHEN YOU DRIVE
JIM DAVIS 3-30

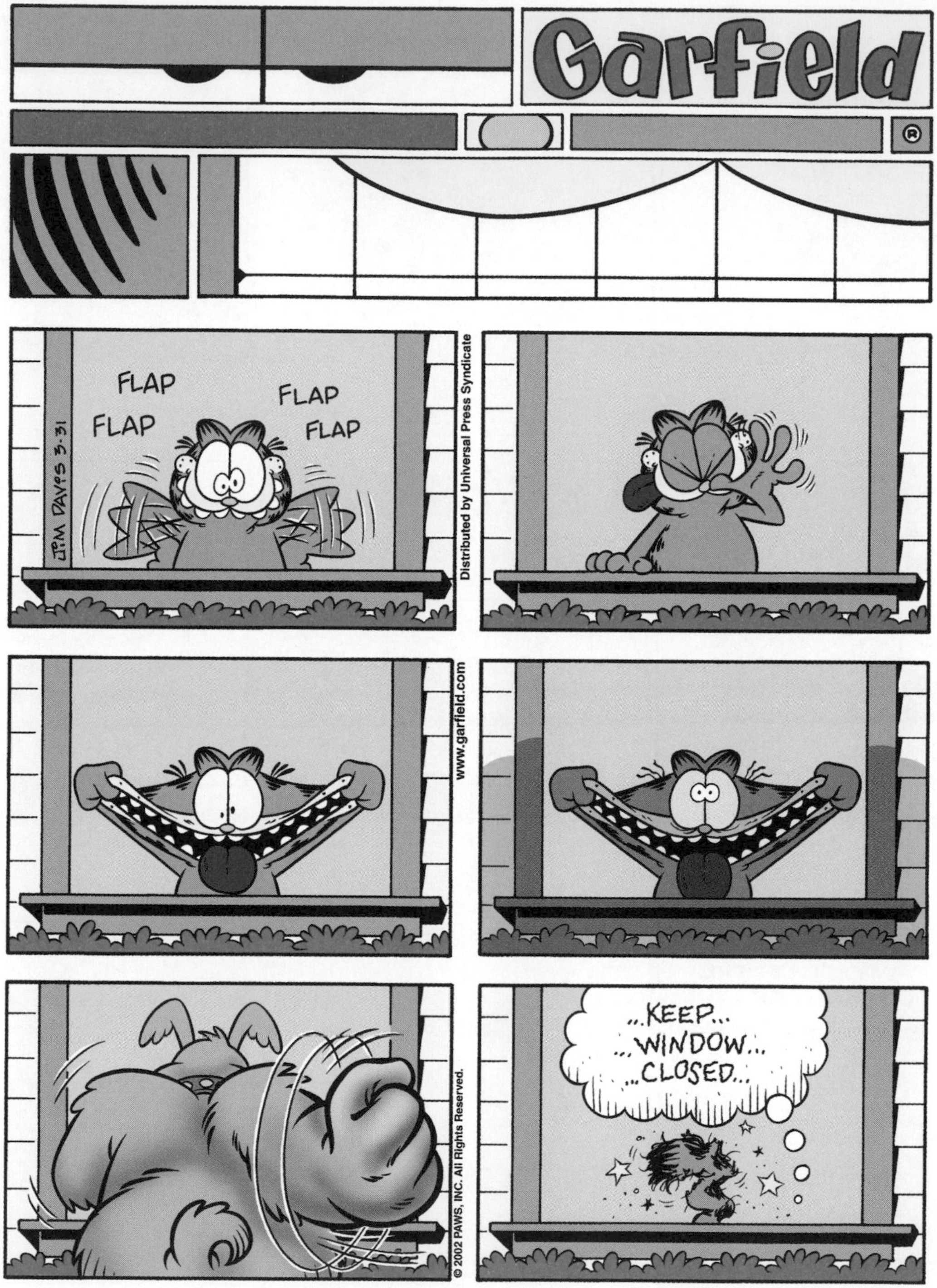
Garfield
FLAP
FLAP
FLAP
FLAP
...KEEP...
...WINDOW...
...CLOSED...
JPM DAVPS 3·31
Distributed by Universal Press Syndicate
www.garfield.com
© 2002 PAWS, INC. All Rights Reserved.

THE ACCORDION IS MY LIFE, GARFIELD
JIM DAVIS 4-1
www.garfield.com
Distributed by Universal Press Syndicate
YOU KNOW WHY?
I DON'T KNOW, JON... WHY?
© 2002 PAWS, INC. All Rights Reserved.
BECAUSE I HAVE SOUL!
NO, JON. YOU HAVE AN ACCORDION

HELLO, SYMPHONY ORCHESTRA?
JIM DAVIS 4-2
www.garfield.com
Distributed by Universal Press Syndicate
I NOTICED YOU DON'T HAVE AN ACCORDION PLAYER
© 2002 PAWS, INC. All Rights Reserved.
YES, I'LL STAY ON THE LINE
WHILE THEY TRACE THE CALL

MY GIRLFRIEND IS ASHAMED TO BE WITH ME
AMEN, BROTHER!
www.garfield.com
Distributed by Universal Press Syndicate
SHE TRIED TO RUN OVER IT WITH HER CAR
I FEEL YOUR PAIN!
JIM DAVIS 4-3
© 2002 PAWS, INC. All Rights Reserved.
BUT I WON'T BE STOPPED!
"ACCORDIONS ANONYMOUS"

I'M THINKING OUR LAWN NEEDS SOMETHING
www.garfield.com Distributed by Universal Press Syndicate
I'M THINKING ABOUT A LAWN ORNAMENT
JIM DAVIS 4-4
© 2002 PAWS, INC. All Rights Reserved.
I'M THINKING OF A TEN-FOOT CONCRETE ACCORDION
I'M THINKING OF MOVING

WHO NEEDS WOMEN, GARFIELD?
JIM DAVIS 4-5
www.garfield.com Distributed by Universal Press Syndicate
ALL WE NEED IS A PAIR OF TINY SHOES, AND...
© 2002 PAWS, INC. All Rights Reserved.
IT'S THE DANCING ACCORDION!
YOU NEED A WOMAN

ACCORDION MUSIC ISN'T JUST MUSIC, GARFIELD
Distributed by Universal Press Syndicate www.garfield.com
IT'S A WAY OF LIFE
© 2002 PAWS, INC. All Rights Reserved.
AND YOU GET TO WEAR LEATHER SHORTS!
LET'S JUST LEAVE IT AT THAT. OKAY, JON?
JIM DAVIS 4-6

GARFIELD®
DINNER WILL BE A LITTLE LATE
THE LASAGNA NEEDS A FEW MORE MINUTES...
THE LASAGNA?!
STAND ASIDE... I'LL BE THE JUDGE OF THIS!
MY SINCEREST APOLOGIES. YOU WERE RIGHT
HEY!
BURP
JIM DAVIS 4-7
Distributed by Universal Press Syndicate
www.garfield.com
© 2002 PAWS, INC. All Rights Reserved.

GARFIELD, LET'S THINK NICE THOUGHTS TODAY
I'M FLOATING ON A CLOUD
I'M BARBECUING A SMALL WOODLAND CREATURE
JIM DAVIS 4-8
www.garfield.com
Distributed by Universal Press Syndicate
© 2002 PAWS, INC. All Rights Reserved.

ODIE, THIS IS GOING TO HURT ME MORE THAN IT WILL YOU
BOOT!
SPLAT!
OR MAYBE NOT...
JIM DAVIS 4-9
www.garfield.com
Distributed by Universal Press Syndicate
© 2002 PAWS, INC. All Rights Reserved.

STILL EATING, GARFIELD?
GARFIELD
SOON YOUR STOMACH WILL GROW LARGE AND YOU WILL EXPLODE
HE'S LIKE AN EVIL FORTUNE COOKIE
GARFIELD
JIM DAVIS 4-10
www.garfield.com
Distributed by Universal Press Syndicate
© 2002 PAWS, INC. All Rights Reserved.

HAVE YOU LOST WEIGHT?
www.garfield.com
Distributed by Universal Press Syndicate
© 2002 PAWS, INC. All Rights Reserved.
YOU BEAST!
JIM DAVIS 4-11

NEWS FLASH! A DERANGED HAMSTER IS TERRORIZING THE CITY!
www.garfield.com
Distributed by Universal Press Syndicate
RESIDENTS ARE ADVISED AGAINST FILLING THEIR POCKETS WITH LETTUCE AND LYING IN TALL GRASS
© 2002 PAWS, INC. All Rights Reserved.
JIM DAVIS 4-12
OH, GREAT!
THERE GOES HIS WEEKEND

DOC, I HAVE A STOMACH ACHE
© 2002 PAWS, INC. All Rights Reserved.
Distributed by Universal Press Syndicate
INDIGESTION?!...
JIM DAVIS 4-13
www.garfield.com
OHHH...SO IT'S **NOT** A PARASITIC ALIEN LIFE FORM BENT ON WORLD CONQUEST?
YOU LIVE ALONE, YOU GET PARANOID

GARFIELD
Distributed by Universal Press Syndicate
BOOT!
www.garfield.com
© 2002 PAWS, INC. All Rights Reserved.
STUPID HEAD WIND
JIM DAVIS 4-14

YOU'RE MORE THAN A PET TO ME, GARFIELD
YOU'RE LIKE A SON
A BIG, FAT, WORTHLESS SON!
LIGHTEN UP, DAD
JIM DAVIS 4-15
Distributed by Universal Press Syndicate www.garfield.com
© 2002 PAWS, INC. All Rights Reserved.

I MAKE A LOT OF THINGS AROUND HERE, GARFIELD
I MAKE THE HOUSE CLEAN. I MAKE THE MEALS...
I MAKE THE BEDS...
AND DON'T FORGET THAT CONTINUAL WHINING SOUND
JIM DAVIS 4-16
Distributed by Universal Press Syndicate www.garfield.com
© 2002 PAWS, INC. All Rights Reserved.

YOU HAVE IT SO EASY!
EASY?... **EASY?!**
I'M WORKING WITHOUT A MATTRESS HERE!
JIM DAVIS 4-17
Distributed by Universal Press Syndicate www.garfield.com
© 2002 PAWS, INC. All Rights Reserved.

LET'S MAKE A LIST OF YOUR FAULTS, GARFIELD
JIM DAVIS 4·18
www.garfield.com
Distributed by Universal Press Syndicate
FAT, LAZY, SELFISH...
AND...
© 2002 PAWS, INC. All Rights Reserved.
AND LET'S NOT FORGET DISRESPECTFUL
MY PERSONAL FAVORITE

WHEN YOU WERE LITTLE, YOU'D LIE ON MY LAP AND PURR
www.garfield.com
Distributed by Universal Press Syndicate
BURP
© 2002 PAWS, INC. All Rights Reserved.
THAT WAS LONG, LOOONG AGO
I'VE MATURED NICELY, DON'T YOU THINK?
JIM DAVIS 4·19

I'M TIRED OF JUST LYING HERE
www.garfield.com
Distributed by Universal Press Syndicate
© 2002 PAWS, INC. All Rights Reserved.
CARRY ME SOMEPLACE ELSE
YANK YANK
JIM DAVIS 4·20

JIM DAVIS 4-21
Distributed by Universal Press Syndicate
HI, I'M A BLUEBERRY MUFFIN AND SEEM TO HAVE LOST MY WAY
EXCUSE ME...
www.garfield.com
I'M A BUTTER PAT AND I'M ALSO LOST...
HI, PAT
PARDON...
© 2002 PAWS, INC. All Rights Reserved.
I'M A STEAMING-HOT CUP OF COFFEE AND I DO BELIEVE I'VE TAKEN A WRONG TURN
EVEN IF THIS **IS** A DREAM, IT'S STILL THE HAPPIEST MOMENT OF MY LIFE
I'M COLD. CAN YOU WARM ME UP?
ME TOO
I'M **BURNING** UP... GOT ANY CREAM?
HEY, PARLEZ-VOUS FRANCAIS, ANYONE?!

I'M PERFECT
YOU'RE A MESS
THAT'S A **PERFECT** MESS, BOZO!
JIM DAVIS 4-22
www.garfield.com
Distributed by Universal Press Syndicate
© 2002 PAWS, INC. All Rights Reserved.

MAYBE SOMEDAY THEY'LL MAKE A MOVIE ABOUT MY LIFE
WHOA...
THOSE POOR STUNT MEN!
JIM DAVIS 4-23
www.garfield.com
Distributed by Universal Press Syndicate
© 2002 PAWS, INC. All Rights Reserved.

HA! HA! HA! HA! HA! HA!
Cat News
JIM DAVIS 4-24
www.garfield.com
Distributed by Universal Press Syndicate
HEY, JON!
CHECK OUT THIS COMIC STRIP ABOUT A FAT, LAZY HUMAN!
© 2002 PAWS, INC. All Rights Reserved.

I WONDER IF GRAVITY IS STILL WORKING
www.garfield.com
Distributed by Universal Press Syndicate
PUSH
© 2002 PAWS, INC. All Rights Reserved.
IT'S NICE TO KNOW THAT THERE ARE SOME THINGS YOU CAN COUNT ON
THUD!
JIM DAVIS 4·25

WOMEN LIKE A MAN OF MYSTERY, SO I'M GOING TO WEAR A MASK ON MY DATE
www.garfield.com
Distributed by Universal Press Syndicate
THIS SHOULD BE A HOOT
© 2002 PAWS, INC. All Rights Reserved.
DON'T WAIT UP
TAKE ME WITH YOU
JIM DAVIS 4·26

READY TO EAT, GARFIELD?
EXCUSE ME?!
JIM DAVIS 4·27
www.garfield.com
Distributed by Universal Press Syndicate
I EAT, I SLEEP. THAT'S ALL I DO. DO I LOOK LIKE I'M SLEEPING?
© 2002 PAWS, INC. All Rights Reserved.
ARE YOU OKAY?
DO YOU SEE A "Z" FLOATING OVER MY HEAD?!

Garfield®
THAT'S ME WITH MY HIGH-SCHOOL CHESS CLUB
AH...
THE JOCKS HATED US
THEY WERE PROBABLY INTIMIDATED BY YOU GUYS
SO ONE DAY I CHALLENGED ONE OF THEM TO A GAME OF CHESS
I SAID, "MAKE THE FIRST MOVE, YOU BIG LUMMOX"
THAT'S WHEN HE SHOVED HIS BISHOP UP MY NOSE
IT'S KIND OF HARD TO TALK ABOUT
NOT HALF AS HARD AS IT IS TO LISTEN TO
JPM DAVIS 4-28
Distributed by Universal Press Syndicate
www.garfield.com
© 2002 PAWS, INC. All Rights Reserved.

SOMEWHERE OUT THERE IS THE WOMAN FOR ME
www.garfield.com
Distributed by Universal Press Syndicate
JIM DAVIS 4-29
© 2002 PAWS, INC. All Rights Reserved.
HIDING, NO DOUBT
THAT WAS MY LINE!

UH-HUH. I SEE. OKAY. MAKES SENSE. ALL RIGHT. I CAN'T ARGUE WITH THAT ONE
© 2002 PAWS, INC. All Rights Reserved.
www.garfield.com
Distributed by Universal Press Syndicate
I HAD NO IDEA THERE WERE SO MANY REASONS NOT TO GO OUT WITH ME
JIM DAVIS 4-30
RING
SHE THOUGHT OF SOME MORE

BESIDES BEAUTY AND INTELLIGENCE...
www.garfield.com
Distributed by Universal Press Syndicate
I NEED A WOMAN WHO WILL RESPECT ME
© 2002 PAWS, INC. All Rights Reserved.
A HUMAN WOMAN?
JIM DAVIS 5-1

EVELYN, SAY YOU'LL GO OUT WITH ME...
JIM DAVIS 5-2
www.garfield.com
Distributed by Universal Press Syndicate
REALLY?! YOU'RE NOT JUST SAYING THAT?!
© 2002 PAWS, INC. All Rights Reserved.
OH, YOU ARE JUST SAYING THAT
NICE SHOT, EVELYN!

I HAVE TO SHOW ELLEN THAT I LOVE ANIMALS AND CHILDREN
www.garfield.com
Distributed by Universal Press Syndicate
SO, I'M TAKING YOU ON MY DATE TONIGHT
© 2002 PAWS, INC. All Rights Reserved.
NOW, WHERE CAN I FIND A KID?
I DON'T WORK WITH CHILDREN
JIM DAVIS 5-3

SHE LOVES ME... SHE LOVES ME NOT...
www.garfield.com
Distributed by Universal Press Syndicate
SHE LOVES ME... SHE DESPISES THE AIR I BREATHE
JIM DAVIS 5-4
© 2002 PAWS, INC. All Rights Reserved.
SHE LOVES ME... SHE WISHES MY HEAD WOULD EXPLODE...
RELAX, JON, RELAX

Garfield
YOUR MOVE
www.garfield.com
JUMP
JUMP
JUMP
Distributed by Universal Press Syndicate
© 2002 PAWS, INC. All Rights Reserved.
IN "CHECKERS WITH COOKIES," THERE **ARE** NO LOSERS
YER MOOF
JPM DAVIS 5-5

GARFIELD!
JIM DAVIS 5-6
Distributed by Universal Press Syndicate www.garfield.com
I THOUGHT YOU WERE GETTING UP!
I AM
© 2002 PAWS, INC. All Rights Reserved.
THIS HAS TO BE DONE IN STAGES

SHADES MAKE YOU LOOK COOL
Distributed by Universal Press Syndicate www.garfield.com
JIM DAVIS 5-7
© 2002 PAWS, INC. All Rights Reserved.
THERE'S NOT A PAIR BIG ENOUGH, PAL!

PET OWNERSHIP IS A TWO-WAY STREET, YOU KNOW
Distributed by Universal Press Syndicate www.garfield.com
I DO EXPECT SOME AFFECTION IN RETURN
NO PROB...
© 2002 PAWS, INC. All Rights Reserved.
ODIE, OWNER, AFFECTION, NOW
JIM DAVIS 5-8

I'LL FEED YOU IN A MINUTE, GARFIELD
Distributed by Universal Press Syndicate www.garfield.com
GARFIELD
GRRR
GRRR
GARFIELD
© 2002 PAWS, INC. All Rights Reserved.
WHAT COULD HE DO? I HAD HIM OUTNUMBERED
JIM DAVIS 5-9
GARFIELD

I HAVE A DILEMMA, GARFIELD. THERE'S A GIRL WHO WANTS TO GO OUT WITH ME SATURDAY NIGHT
Distributed by Universal Press Syndicate www.garfield.com
AND SHE HAS A FACE THAT COULD STOP A CLOCK
© 2002 PAWS, INC. All Rights Reserved.
SO, WHAT SHOULD I WEAR?
WELL, DON'T WEAR YOUR WATCH
JIM DAVIS 5-10

A CAT IS CONSTANTLY ON THE MOVE
Distributed by Universal Press Syndicate www.garfield.com
© 2002 PAWS, INC. All Rights Reserved.
I DON'T PERSONALLY KNOW THIS CAT, BUT I'VE HEARD OF HIM
JIM DAVIS 5-11

garfield®
www.garfield.com
Distributed by Universal Press Syndicate
© 2002 PAWS, INC. All Rights Reserved.
MADE YOU LOOK!
JIM DAVIS 5-12

THERE'S OUR COW, BOSSIE. SHE KICKED ME IN THE HEAD ONCE
SHE KICKED ME IN THE HEAD ONCE
COMES THE DAWN...
PHOTOS
JIM DAVIS 5-13
Distributed by Universal Press Syndicate www.garfield.com
© 2002 PAWS, INC. All Rights Reserved.

...AND THIS IS A PICTURE OF MY PRIZE ROOSTER, HENRY
THAT'S A PICTURE OF AN EGG
HE WAS MUCH YOUNGER THEN
AH...
BUT HE ALREADY HAD HIS DAD'S RUGGED GOOD LOOKS
YOU'RE SCARING ME, JON
JIM DAVIS 5-14
Distributed by Universal Press Syndicate www.garfield.com
© 2002 PAWS, INC. All Rights Reserved.

WE HAD TO MAKE OUR OWN FUN BACK ON THE FARM...
DOC BOY AND I USED TO PLAY A GAME WITH THE ELECTRIC FENCE WE CALLED "TOUCH IT, WIMP!"
MY FINGERS STILL TINGLE
AND THE BRAIN'S STILL NUMB
JIM DAVIS 5-15
Distributed by Universal Press Syndicate www.garfield.com
© 2002 PAWS, INC. All Rights Reserved.

I REMEMBER BACK ON THE FARM... MY MOTHER CALLING TO ME...
"JON, YOU'RE BORING THE CATTLE!"
EVER SEE A COW YAWN?
NOW YOU'RE BORING THE CAT
JIM DAVIS 5-16
www.garfield.com
Distributed by Universal Press Syndicate
© 2002 PAWS, INC. All Rights Reserved.

MOM SET ME UP ON A BLIND DATE WITH A GIRL FROM BACK ON THE FARM
JIM DAVIS 5-17
SHE CHURNS HER OWN BUTTER...
...AND HAS A WONDERFUL SENSE OF HUMOR
AND HAS A WONDERFUL SENSE OF HUMOR!
www.garfield.com
Distributed by Universal Press Syndicate
© 2002 PAWS, INC. All Rights Reserved.

GARFIELD, A LETTER FROM HOME!
JIM DAVIS 5-18
JUST WHEN I WAS FEELING DOWN, TOO
"DEAR SON, THE ENTIRE FAMILY FELL OFF THE ROOF"
I DON'T EVEN WANT TO KNOW...
www.garfield.com
Distributed by Universal Press Syndicate
© 2002 PAWS, INC. All Rights Reserved.

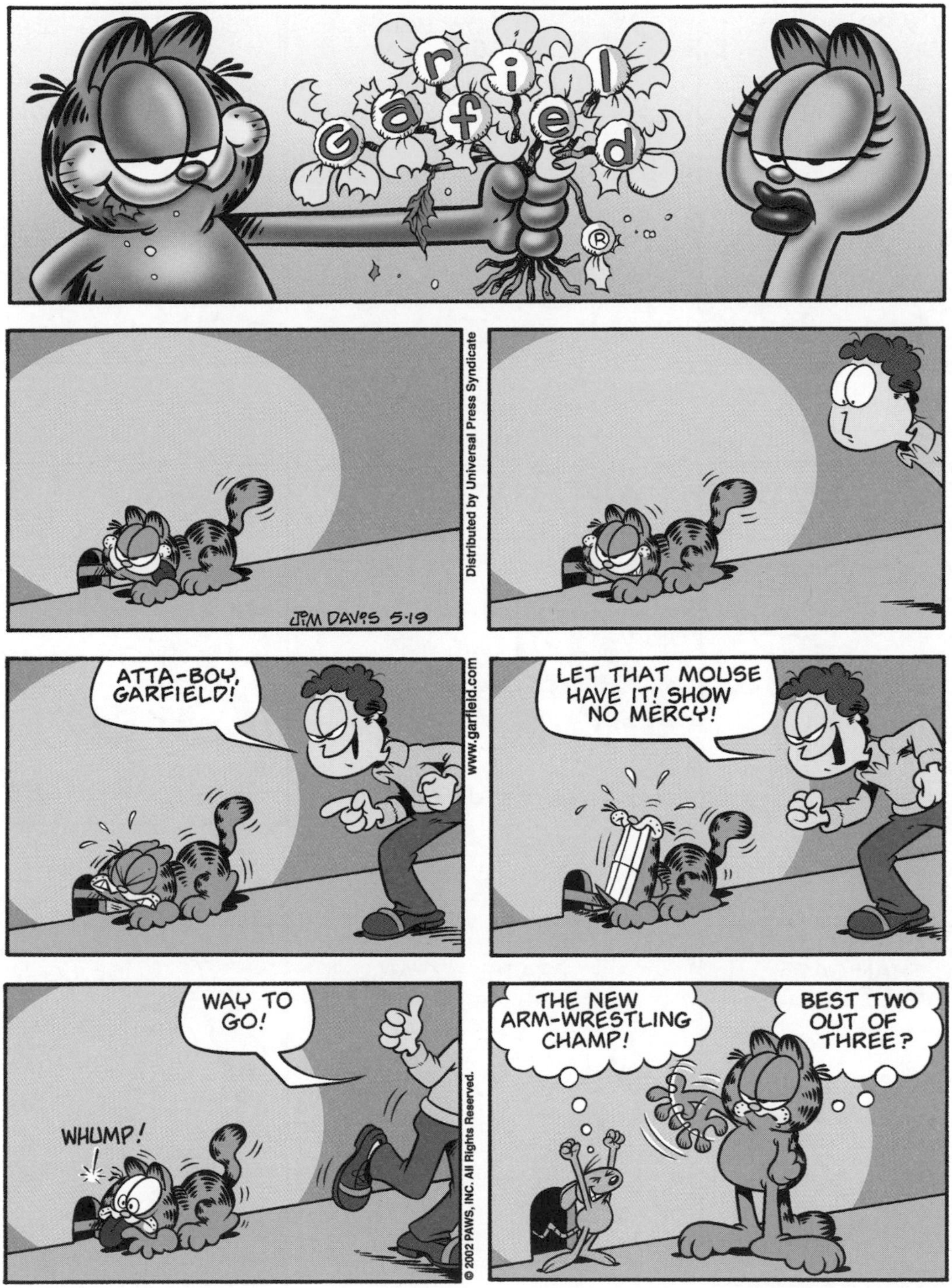
Garfield ®
JIM DAVIS 5-19
Distributed by Universal Press Syndicate
ATTA-BOY, GARFIELD!
www.garfield.com
LET THAT MOUSE HAVE IT! SHOW NO MERCY!
WAY TO GO!
WHUMP!
© 2002 PAWS, INC. All Rights Reserved.
THE NEW ARM-WRESTLING CHAMP!
BEST TWO OUT OF THREE?

© 2002 PAWS, INC. All Rights Reserved.
I KNOW WHY YOU'RE SO LAZY, GARFIELD
www.garfield.com
Distributed by Universal Press Syndicate
LOW SELF-ESTEEM
JIM DAVIS 5-20
YOU HAVE TO REALIZE YOUR WORTH
DID I SAY YOU COULD SPEAK?

I'M RUNNING IN PLACE!
JIM DAVIS 5-21
www.garfield.com
I'M JUST STANDING HERE
Distributed by Universal Press Syndicate
AND I'M WINNING
© 2002 PAWS, INC. All Rights Reserved.

KNOW WHY HUMANS ARE SMARTER THAN CATS, GARFIELD?
© 2002 PAWS, INC. All Rights Reserved.
www.garfield.com
BIGGER BRAINS
AH...
Distributed by Universal Press Syndicate
THAT EXPLAINS THOSE HUGE, UGLY HEADS
JIM DAVIS 5-22

YIP! YIP! YAP! YIP! YIP! YIP! YIP! YIP! YIP! YIP!
ODIE, IF YOU'LL SHUT UP, I'LL GIVE YOU A PIECE OF CANDY
YIP! YIP! YAP! YIP! YIP! YIP! YIP! YIP! YIP! YIP!
JIM DAVIS 5-23
© 2002 PAWS, INC. All Rights Reserved.
www.garfield.com
Distributed by Universal Press Syndicate

MARCIE, GIVE ME ONE GOOD REASON WHY YOU WON'T GO OUT WITH ME
I SEE
SHE HATES, LOATHES, AND IS DISGUSTED BY EVERY FIBER OF MY BEING
I'LL MARK HER DOWN AS A POSSIBLE
JIM DAVIS 5-24
© 2002 PAWS, INC. All Rights Reserved.
www.garfield.com
Distributed by Universal Press Syndicate

WOULD YOU LIKE TO SEE ME JUGGLE FLAMING CHAIN SAWS BLINDFOLDED?
OR HEAR ME SING?
THE FIRST ONE!!
DOGS DON'T GET TO VOTE
JIM DAVIS 5-25
© 2002 PAWS, INC. All Rights Reserved.
www.garfield.com
Distributed by Universal Press Syndicate

Garfield®
Distributed by Universal Press Syndicate
www.garfield.com
© 2002 PAWS, INC. All Rights Reserved.
*TRIP*
SPLAT!
GRACEFUL
JIM DAVIS 5-26

I'M HERE! LET THE PARTY BEGIN!
SMACK!
I'LL OPEN THE CHIPS
JIM DAVIS 5-27
Distributed by Universal Press Syndicate www.garfield.com
© 2002 PAWS, INC. All Rights Reserved.

FEAR ME, CAT! FEAR MY WRATH! FEAR MY MIGHT!
WHAP!
FEAR MY FLATNESS!
JIM DAVIS 5-28
Distributed by Universal Press Syndicate www.garfield.com
© 2002 PAWS, INC. All Rights Reserved.

YOUR HUSBAND'S A CELEBRITY NOW
PARDON ME?
YEAH, I SAW HIM ON THE FRONT PAGE OF THE NEWSPAPER
REALLY?!
MORTY!
FAME IS FLEETING
JIM DAVIS 5-29
Distributed by Universal Press Syndicate www.garfield.com
© 2002 PAWS, INC. All Rights Reserved.

www.garfield.com
Distributed by Universal Press Syndicate
JIM DAVIS 5-30
© 2002 PAWS, INC. All Rights Reserved.
NEW HAT?
THANKS FOR NOTICING

HERE'S A PICTURE OF MY KIDS
www.garfield.com
Distributed by Universal Press Syndicate
WHOA, THEY'RE DISGUSTING!
© 2002 PAWS, INC. All Rights Reserved.
WHY, THANK YOU!
JIM DAVIS 5-31

...AND THAT'S THE STORY OF MY LIFE
JIM DAVIS 6-1
www.garfield.com
Distributed by Universal Press Syndicate
SMACK!
© 2002 PAWS, INC. All Rights Reserved.
THE END

Garfield
GRUNKA
GRUNKA
GRUNKA
Distributed by Universal Press Syndicate
GRUNKA
GRUNKA
GRUNKA
GRUNKA
GRUNKA
GRUNKA
www.garfield.com
GRUNKA
GRUNKA
GRUNKA
© 2002 PAWS, INC. All Rights Reserved.
GRUNKA
GRUNKA
GRUNKA
JPM DAVIS 6-2

YAWN
STRETCH
BURP
SCRATCH
SCRATCH
SCRATCH
BUSY?
DON'T GET ME STARTED
JIM DAVIS 6-3
www.garfield.com
Distributed by Universal Press Syndicate
© 2002 PAWS, INC. All Rights Reserved.

I'M AT A POINT IN MY LIFE WHEN IT'S TIME TO ASK MYSELF THE HARD QUESTIONS, GARFIELD
LIKE, CAN TOADS GIVE WARTS TO EACH OTHER?
OW! OW! NOW MY HEAD HURTS!
SHOULD'VE STARTED WITH AN EASIER ONE
JIM DAVIS 6-4
www.garfield.com
Distributed by Universal Press Syndicate
© 2002 PAWS, INC. All Rights Reserved.

I'M WEARING MY BOXER SHORTS BACKWARDS!
I HAD A FEELING SOMETHING BIG WAS GOING TO HAPPEN TODAY
JIM DAVIS 6-5
www.garfield.com
Distributed by Universal Press Syndicate
© 2002 PAWS, INC. All Rights Reserved.

I HAVE A LOT ON MY MIND
GOOD
MAYBE THAT'LL KEEP IT FROM BLOWING AWAY
JIM DAVIS 6-6
© 2002 PAWS, INC. All Rights Reserved
Distributed by Universal Press Syndicate www.garfield.com

I HAVE A DATE TONIGHT, GARFIELD
YOU KNOW WHAT THAT MEANS...
SOMETIME TODAY I'LL GET A HUGE PIMPLE!
A TIME-HONORED TRADITION
JIM DAVIS 6-7
Distributed by Universal Press Syndicate www.garfield.com
© 2002 PAWS, INC. All Rights Reserved.

WE CANCEL EACH OTHER OUT
JIM DAVIS 6-8
Distributed by Universal Press Syndicate www.garfield.com
© 2002 PAWS, INC. All Rights Reserved.

GARFIELD®
WHY DON'T THE CHICKS DIG ME, GARFIELD? ...MAYBE IF I-
JIM DAVIS 6-9
Distributed by Universal Press Syndicate
www.garfield.com
WAR AND PEACE
18
Estimated download time : 7.32 hours
© 2002 PAWS, INC. All Rights Reserved.
...OR MAYBE IF I SHAVED MY HEAD AND GLUED ALL THE HAIR ONTO MY CHEST
DID I MISS ANYTHING?

SO I'LL BE 24 SOON...THAT'S A NICE NUMBER
A NICE BIG, FAT, INCREDIBLY HUGE, HONKING NUMBER
JIM DAVIS 6-10
www.garfield.com Distributed by Universal Press Syndicate
© 2002 PAWS, INC. All Rights Reserved.

I'M TURNING 24 NEXT WEEK...
DO YOU KNOW WHAT I HATE MOST ABOUT MY BIRTHDAY?
-CUE THE ANSWER
HI! I'M NERMAL. THE WORLD'S CUTEST KITTEN!
JIM DAVIS 6-11
www.garfield.com Distributed by Universal Press Syndicate
© 2002 PAWS, INC. All Rights Reserved.

I'M CURIOUS. WHEN YOU'RE AS OLD AS YOU ARE...
JIM DAVIS 6-12
WHAT GOES FIRST? THE MEMORY? THE EYES? THE BACK?
THE KITTEN
www.garfield.com Distributed by Universal Press Syndicate
© 2002 PAWS, INC. All Rights Reserved.

SO I HEAR YOU'RE GOING TO BE 24
THIS IS TRUE
© 2002 PAWS, INC. All Rights Reserved.
Distributed by Universal Press Syndicate
WOW! THE THINGS YOU'VE BEEN WITNESS TO!
www.garfield.com
JIM DAVIS 6-13
WHAT **WAS** LIFE LIKE BEFORE FAX MACHINES?!
IT'S TOO HORRIFIC TO DESCRIBE

HOW DO YOU INTEND TO CELEBRATE YOUR BIRTHDAY?
WHAT DO YOU MEAN?
© 2002 PAWS, INC. All Rights Reserved.
Distributed by Universal Press Syndicate
WELL...
JIM DAVIS 6-14
www.garfield.com
ARE YOU GONNA WHEEZE OUT A FEW CANDLES?
RUN FOR YOUR LIFE

SO I'LL SOON BE 24. THAT MEANS I WILL BE OLDER AND WISER...
© 2002 PAWS, INC. All Rights Reserved.
HA! HA! HA! HA!
Distributed by Universal Press Syndicate
www.garfield.com
JIM DAVIS 6-15
I'LL BE OLDER

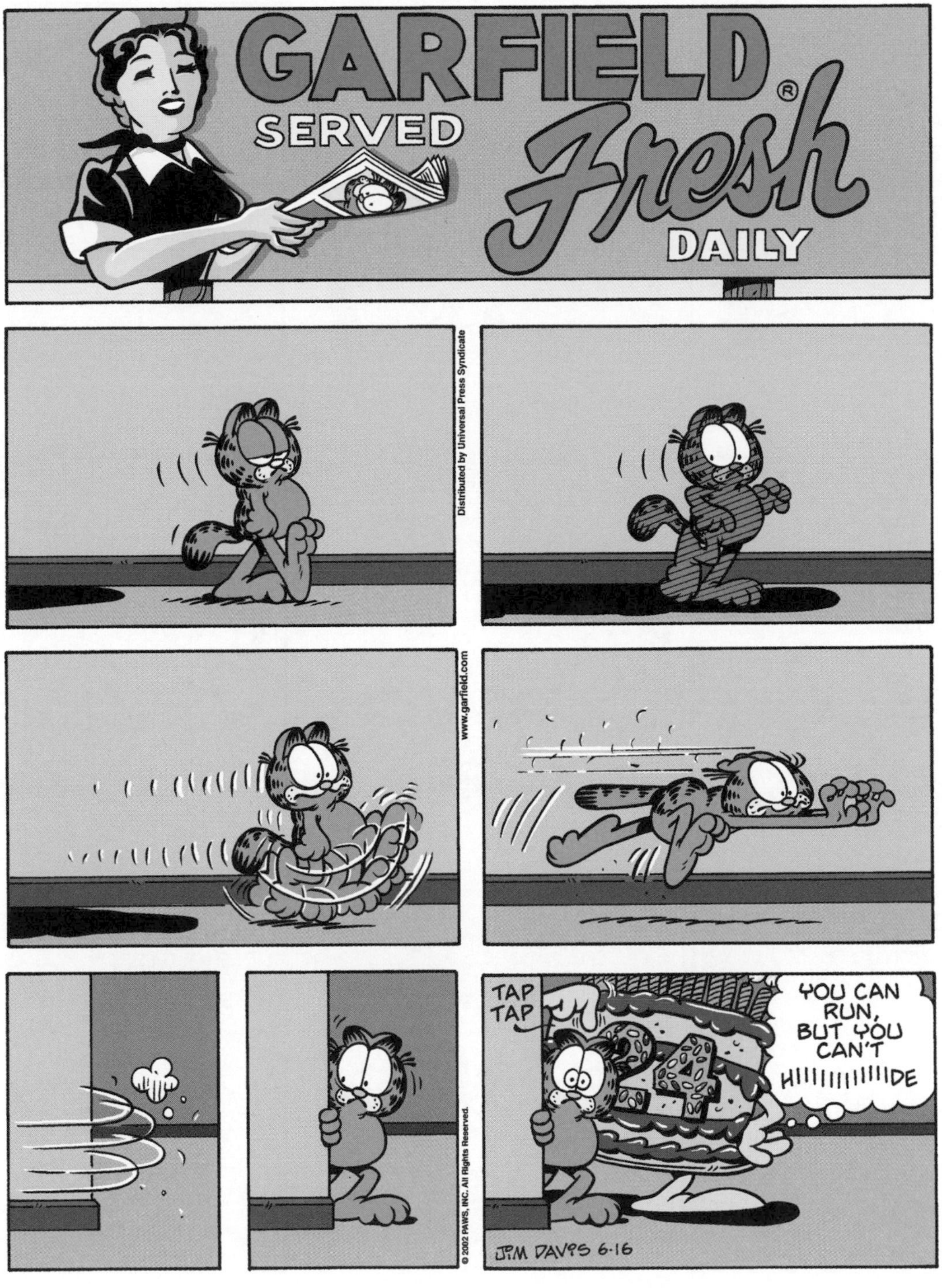
GARFIELD®
SERVED
Fresh
DAILY
TAP TAP
YOU CAN RUN, BUT YOU CAN'T HIIIIIIIIIIIDE
JPM DAVPS 6-16
Distributed by Universal Press Syndicate
www.garfield.com
© 2002 PAWS, INC. All Rights Reserved.

I'M GOING TO BE 24 SOON
AND THAT LOOK YOU'RE GIVING ME ISN'T HELPING
JIM DAVIS 6-17
www.garfield.com
Distributed by Universal Press Syndicate
© 2002 PAWS, INC. All Rights Reserved.

24 YEARS IS A LONG TIME. WHAT'S THE SECRET TO YOUR LONGEVITY?
I SEEEEEEE...
WAIT, WAIT, THERE'S MORE
www.garfield.com
Distributed by Universal Press Syndicate
JIM DAVIS 6-18
© 2002 PAWS, INC. All Rights Reserved.

JIM DAVIS 6-19
www.garfield.com
Distributed by Universal Press Syndicate
HAPPY BIRTHDAY, BIG GUY!
I'M NOT EATING THAT
© 2002 PAWS, INC. All Rights Reserved.

YOU SHOULD DO SOME SIT-UPS
I DON'T KNOW...
IT MIGHT CAUSE ME TO SPILL MY MILKSHAKE
JIM DAVIS 6-20
www.garfield.com
Distributed by Universal Press Syndicate
© 2002 PAWS, INC. All Rights Reserved.

AHA! HE CAN ONLY GET HIS HAND OUT IF HE LETS GO OF THE COOKIE
WHAT WILL HE DO?
HE WILL USE HIS WITS AND YOUR HEAD
COOKIES
JIM DAVIS 6-21
www.garfield.com
Distributed by Universal Press Syndicate
© 2002 PAWS, INC. All Rights Reserved.

YOU KNOW BETTER THAN TO STAND BETWEEN ME AND THE KITCHEN WHEN IT'S SNACK TIME
JIM DAVIS 6-22
www.garfield.com
Distributed by Universal Press Syndicate
© 2002 PAWS, INC. All Rights Reserved.

GARFIELD®
IT'S GARFIELD!
OH SURE, LAY THE PRESSURE ON ME!
DO YOU REALIZE ALL THE RESPONSIBILITY THAT IS ATTENDANT TO BEING GARFIELD?!
THE EATING OF FOOD?! THE TAKING OF NAPS?! THE KICKING OF ODIE?!
WHY CAN'T I BE YOU?...ALL CAREFREE AND SILLY?
HYUH! HYUH! HYUH!
COMPLEX LITTLE CREATURES, AREN'T THEY?
JIM DAVIS 6-23
www.garfield.com
Distributed by Universal Press Syndicate
© 2002 PAWS, INC. All Rights Reserved.

IT SAYS HERE THAT PETS CAN BE A REAL COMFORT
JIM DAVIS 6-24
SO COMFORT ME!
GET A FLEECY BLANKET
Distributed by Universal Press Syndicate www.garfield.com
© 2002 PAWS, INC. All Rights Reserved.

SAYS HERE THAT CATS AND LIONS ARE IN THE SAME FAMILY
JIM DAVIS 6-25
YOU MUST BE ADOPTED
HEY!
Distributed by Universal Press Syndicate www.garfield.com
© 2002 PAWS, INC. All Rights Reserved.

SNIP SNIP SNIP SNIP SNIP SNIP SNIP SNIP SNIP SNIP SNIP SNIP
I'LL LET YOU KNOW IF I SEE A CAT FOOD COUPON, OKAY?!
JIM DAVIS 6-26
Distributed by Universal Press Syndicate www.garfield.com
© 2002 PAWS, INC. All Rights Reserved.

THERE'S GOING TO BE A PET SHOW NEXT WEEK, GARFIELD
HMMM
www.garfield.com
Distributed by Universal Press Syndicate
BIG PRIZES!
SOUNDS INTERESTING
© 2002 PAWS, INC. All Rights Reserved.
WE SHOULD ENTER!
VERY WELL. GO FETCH YOUR LEASH, BOY
JIM DAVIS 6-27

"THEN THE ZOMBIE CAME CLOSER AND CLOSER!"
LAME...
SCARY STORIES
www.garfield.com
Distributed by Universal Press Syndicate
"THEN HE BROKE DOWN THE DOOR AND WALKED INTO THE HOUSE"
OOOH... I'M SO SCARED
JIM DAVIS 6-28
© 2002 PAWS, INC. All Rights Reserved.
"AND HE ATE THE LAST OF THE ROAST TURKEY"
OH, NO!!!

"PETS ARE VERY SENSITIVE"
PETS
JIM DAVIS 6-29
www.garfield.com
Distributed by Universal Press Syndicate
"MAKE SURE YOU GIVE THEM PLENTY OF HUGS"
© 2002 PAWS, INC. All Rights Reserved.
C'MERE, MISTER SENSITIVE!
TOUCH ME AND I'LL REMOVE YOUR ARMS

garfield
Distributed by Universal Press Syndicate
© 2002 PAWS, INC. All Rights Reserved.
www.garfield.com
YOU BLINKED... I WIN!
JIM DAVIS 6·30

JIM DAVIS 7-1
Distributed by Universal Press Syndicate www.garfield.com
RATTLE RATTLE
© 2002 PAWS, INC. All Rights Reserved.
A TUNNEL?!
KILL THE LIGHTS!

GARFIELD, HAVE YOU **EVER** EATEN UNTIL YOU WERE ACTUALLY FULL?
FULL?
GARFIELD
Distributed by Universal Press Syndicate www.garfield.com
FUUULL...
GARFIELD
© 2002 PAWS, INC. All Rights Reserved.
NO COMPRENDO, SEÑOR
I DIDN'T THINK SO
GARFIELD
JIM DAVIS 7-2

GARFIELD, YOU ATE ALL THE PIE!
JIM DAVIS 7-3
Distributed by Universal Press Syndicate www.garfield.com
YOU COULD AT LEAST LOOK SORRY!
© 2002 PAWS, INC. All Rights Reserved.
OOPS, SOMETIMES I GET MY "SORRY" LOOK MIXED UP WITH MY "NO-PIE-FOR-YOU" LOOK

I'M DEPRESSED...
BUT WAIT! THERE'S A LIGHT AT THE END OF THE TUNNEL!
Distributed by Universal Press Syndicate www.garfield.com
JPM DAVPS 7-4
© 2002 PAWS, INC. All Rights Reserved.
COOKIES

GARFIELD... GARFIELD!
GULP
CHOMP
SNARF
GULP
THERE'S NO FOOD ON THAT PLATE
JON, JON, JON. WHEN YOU'RE AT THE TOP OF YOUR GAME, YOU HAVE TO TRAIN EVEN HARDER
JPM DAVPS 7-5
Distributed by Universal Press Syndicate www.garfield.com
© 2002 PAWS, INC. All Rights Reserved.

LUNCH
GARFIELD
GULP
GARFIELD
DINNER
TRAINING AN OWNER IS HARD WORK, BUT THE BENEFITS ARE GREAT
GARF
JPM DAVPS 7-6
Distributed by Universal Press Syndicate www.garfield.com
© 2002 PAWS, INC. All Rights Reserved.

GARFIELD
GARFIELD! BREAKFAST!!
YAWN
STRETCH
Distributed by Universal Press Syndicate
www.garfield.com
STRETCH
MMMMM MMMMM
...ONE FORK, EXTRA LONG, PLEASE
GARFIELD
JIM DAVIS 7-7

I WONDER IF IT'S POSSIBLE FOR YOU TO BE MORE SPOILED THAN YOU ARE
JIM DAVIS 7-8
Distributed by Universal Press Syndicate www.garfield.com
MORE SPOILED?
© 2002 PAWS, INC. All Rights Reserved.
FOR YOU, I'LL TRY!

LOOK AT THAT
Distributed by Universal Press Syndicate www.garfield.com
ONLY THINKING OF THEMSELVES
BSU
© 2002 PAWS, INC. All Rights Reserved.
JIM DAVIS 7-9
I HAVE TO DO THE RELAXING FOR ALL THREE OF US

YOU SLEEP TOO MUCH
YOU TALK TOO MUCH
Distributed by Universal Press Syndicate www.garfield.com
AND YOU'RE A LUMP
YOU'RE A DORK
© 2002 PAWS, INC. All Rights Reserved.
BUT I LOVE YOU ANYWAY
YOU'RE STILL A DORK
JIM DAVIS 7-10

MY FOOT'S ASLEEP
JIM DAVIS 7-11
Distributed by Universal Press Syndicate www.garfield.com
© 2002 PAWS, INC. All Rights Reserved.

HELLO, COMPLAINT DEPARTMENT?... I HAVE A COMPLAINT
MY TOASTER IS BROKEN...
AND MY LIFE STINKS!
IS IT UNDER WARRANTY?
JIM DAVIS 7-12
Distributed by Universal Press Syndicate www.garfield.com
© 2002 PAWS, INC. All Rights Reserved.

IF MOM HAD ADDED A HOLE FOR MY HEAD, THIS WOULD BE MY FAVORITE SWEATER
SO, LET ME GET THIS STRAIGHT...
THIS IS YOUR SECOND-FAVORITE SWEATER?
JIM DAVIS 7-13
Distributed by Universal Press Syndicate www.garfield.com
© 2002 PAWS, INC. All Rights Reserved.

GARFIELD®
IT SAYS HERE THAT DOGS PANT TO COOL THEMSELVES
Distributed by Universal Press Syndicate
I SUPPOSE IT'S WORTH A TRY...
WHY NOT?
PANT PANT PANT PANT
PANT PANT PANT
JPM DAVPS 7-14
www.garfield.com
PANT PANT PANT PANT
WHOA, I'M GOING TO HYPERVENTILATE!
PANT PANT PANT PANT
© 2002 PAWS, INC. All Rights Reserved.
PANT PANT PANT PANT PANT PANT PAN-
EASY THERE, JON!
KLUNK
DON'T BELIEVE EVERYTHING YOU READ
SLUK
BZZZZZ

IT'S MONDAY, AND THERE'S NOTHING OVER THERE...
-AND NOTHING OVER THERE...
WHICH CAN ONLY MEAN...
JIM DAVIS 7-15
www.garfield.com Distributed by Universal Press Syndicate
© 2002 PAWS, INC. All Rights Reserved.

WHAT A DARK AND GLOOMY DAY
JIM DAVIS 7-16
ODIE GOT HIS TONGUE STUCK IN THE VACUUM CLEANER, AND ALL HE CAN SAY IS, "AUWL! AUWL!"
CLOUDS PART... THE SUN BREAKS THROUGH...
www.garfield.com Distributed by Universal Press Syndicate
© 2002 PAWS, INC. All Rights Reserved.

NOTHING COULD TAKE THE DULL OUT OF THIS DAY
THIS ISN'T A TIE! IT'S A SNAKE!
BUT, WHAT DO I KNOW?
JIM DAVIS 7-17
www.garfield.com Distributed by Universal Press Syndicate
© 2002 PAWS, INC. All Rights Reserved.

DING-
DONG
DING-
DONG
DING-
DONG
JIM DAVIS 7-18
www.garfield.com
Distributed by Universal Press Syndicate
WHY DON'T YOU USE THE PET DOOR?!
FORGOT THE SECURITY CODE
© 2002 PAWS, INC. All Rights Reserved.

CINDY, I THINK I'M IN LOVE WITH YOU
© 2002 PAWS, INC. All Rights Reserved.
Distributed by Universal Press Syndicate
THE THOUGHT OF YOU MAKES ME SWEAT
JIM DAVIS 7-19
www.garfield.com
WE'RE TALKIN' SOCK-SOAKIN' SWEAT, CINDY!
HE SHOULD WRITE GREETING CARDS

© 2002 PAWS, INC. All Rights Reserved.
Distributed by Universal Press Syndicate
www.garfield.com
WHEW...
JIM DAVIS 7-20
TRAPDOOR DOOOGGG!
TDD

Garfield
DINNERTIME!
WHO WANTS A NICE, REFRESHING GLASS OF LUKEWARM TAP WATER?
YESIREE, CLEANSES THE SYSTEM, HYDRATES THE BODY, RETURNS THAT YOUTHFUL GLOW TO THE SKIN... NATURE'S ENERGY DRINK...
-YUM!
FORGETTING TO SHOP IS NO EXCUSE
SORRY
JIM DAVIS 7-21
www.garfield.com
Distributed by Universal Press Syndicate
© 2002 PAWS, INC. All Rights Reserved.

IS THE DOG HERE?
BEWARE OF THE DOG
HANG ON, I'LL CHECK
HEEEY, WAIT A SECOND. **I'M** THE DOG
SORRY. I MISTOOK YOU FOR THE BUFFOON
JPM DAVPS 7-22
www.garfield.com
Distributed by Universal Press Syndicate
© 2002 PAWS, INC. All Rights Reserved.

I COULD BITE YOU IN HALF WITH MY POWERFUL JAWS!
IF I HADN'T BURNED MY LIPS ON A HOT CAPPUCCINO
YOU'RE PATHETIC
JPM DAVPS 7-23
www.garfield.com
Distributed by Universal Press Syndicate
© 2002 PAWS, INC. All Rights Reserved.

BEWARE OF THE DOG, INC.
BEWARE OF THE DOG, INC.
I CAN'T BARK AT YOU IF YOU DON'T HAVE THE PROPER PAPER WORK
IT'S COME TO THIS!
JPM DAVPS 7-24
www.garfield.com
Distributed by Universal Press Syndicate
© 2002 PAWS, INC. All Rights Reserved.

GRRRRRR
JIM DAVIS 7-25
© 2002 PAWS, INC. All Rights Reserved.
SORRY I'M LATE! DID I MISS ANYTHING?
Distributed by Universal Press Syndicate www.garfield.com
OH, JUST SOME GROWLING AND A LITTLE TEETH GNASHING
DARN! WOULD YOU START OVER, PLEASE?

I CAN'T STAND THE SIGHT OF YOU!
Distributed by Universal Press Syndicate www.garfield.com
THEN I'LL LEAVE
THANK YOU
JIM DAVIS 7-26 © 2002 PAWS, INC. All Rights Reserved.
EEEERRRRGGGGHHHH
Love, Garfield

GRRR. SNARL. BARK
Distributed by Universal Press Syndicate www.garfield.com
YOU CALL THAT THREATENING?
JIM DAVIS 7-27 © 2002 PAWS, INC. All Rights Reserved.
I'M A LITTLE SELF-CONSCIOUS ABOUT MY NEW BRACES
WHAT IS **HAPPENING** WITH THIS WORLD?!

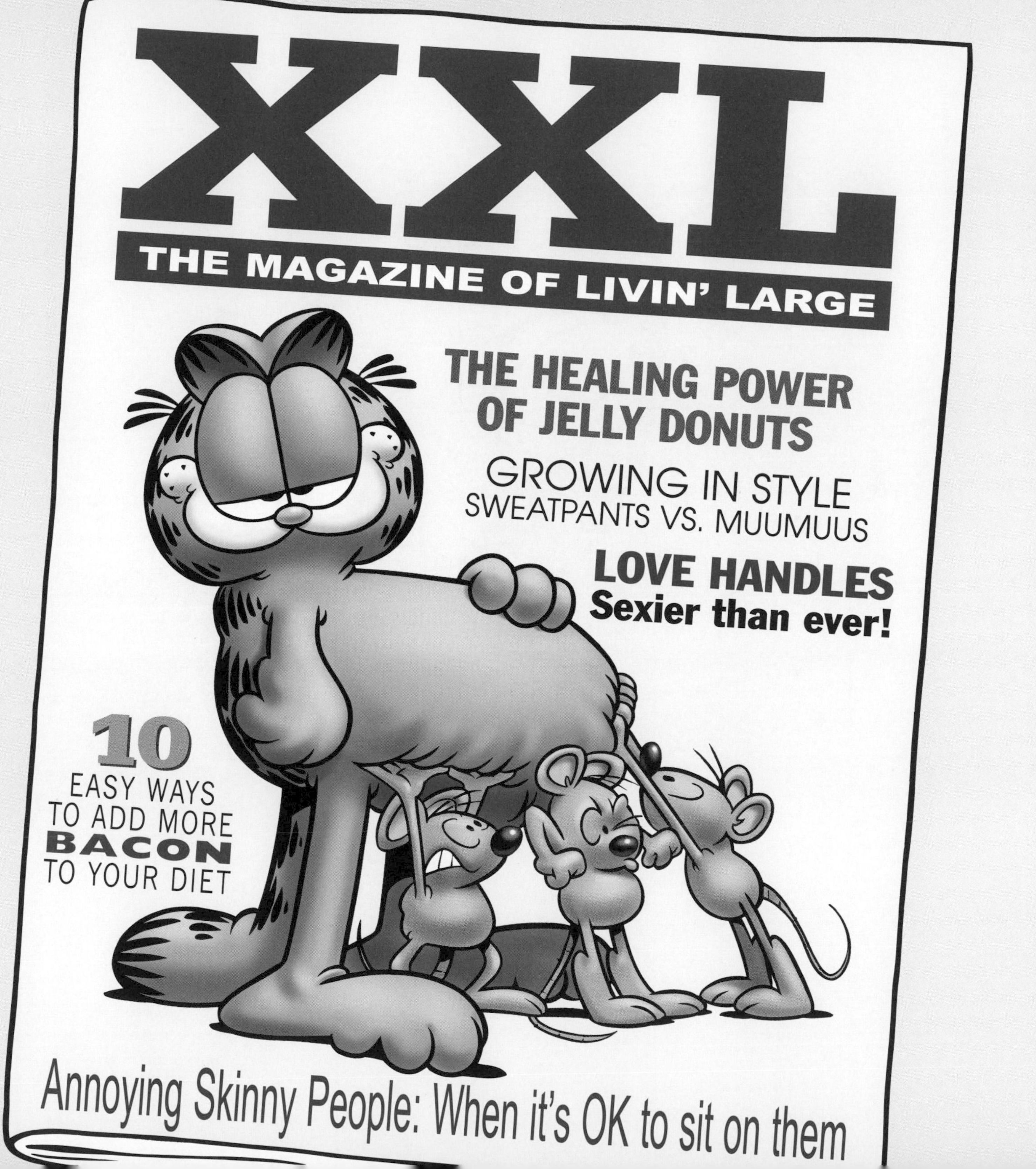
XXL
THE MAGAZINE OF LIVIN' LARGE
THE HEALING POWER OF JELLY DONUTS
GROWING IN STYLE
SWEATPANTS VS. MUUMUUS
LOVE HANDLES
Sexier than ever!
10 EASY WAYS TO ADD MORE BACON TO YOUR DIET
Annoying Skinny People: When it's OK to sit on them

SNACK BREAK!

# Garfield
# PIGS OUT

BY JIM DAVIS

Ballantine Books • New York

Fun with Spiders!
Tic-Whack-Toe
Paiñata
Go Squish
Dunk Tank
Big, Flat, Hairy Deal

GARFIELD
PEANUT B
TUNA
GULP
PORK AND BEANS
GOBBLE GOBBLE GOBBLE
POTATO STICKS
CRUNCH CRUNCH CRUNCH
APPLE PIE FILLING
SLUP SLUP
TOMATO PASTE
SLURP!
YOU HAVE BEEN WATCHING "EATING STUFF OUT OF CANS"
COOKING SHOW THEMES ARE RUNNING THIN
JIM DAVIS 7-28
www.garfield.com
© 2002 PAWS, INC. All Rights Reserved.
Distributed by Universal Press Syndicate

BEING AROUND ME MUST BE FUN
I WANT TO GET IN ON SOME OF THAT!
JIM DAVIS 7-29
www.garfield.com
Distributed by Universal Press Syndicate
© 2002 PAWS, INC. All Rights Reserved.

THIS IS THE WORST HAMBURGER IN THE HISTORY OF HAMBURGERS!
ZWIP
I'VE FILCHED WORSE
JIM DAVIS 7-30
www.garfield.com
Distributed by Universal Press Syndicate
© 2002 PAWS, INC. All Rights Reserved.

I ONCE DATED A MODEL, GARFIELD
CINDY KROVITZ
SHE WAS A COVER GIRL FOR "BARBERSHOP DIGEST"
NICE HANDLEBAR MOUSTACHE
JIM DAVIS 7-31
www.garfield.com
Distributed by Universal Press Syndicate
© 2002 PAWS, INC. All Rights Reserved.

THERE THEY ARE, GARFIELD
JIM DAVIS 8-1
www.garfield.com Distributed by Universal Press Syndicate
IT'S BEEN A LONG TIME, HASN'T IT?
© 2002 PAWS, INC. All Rights Reserved.
THAT'S THE LAST TIME I TAKE PICTURES OF YOUR FEET
THEY'VE GROWN SO

YOU DON'T REMEMBER ME?
JIM DAVIS 8-2
www.garfield.com Distributed by Universal Press Syndicate
WE WENT OUT ON A DATE LAST NIGHT
© 2002 PAWS, INC. All Rights Reserved.
DOESN'T RING A BELL?
I'M SURE IT'LL COME OUT IN THERAPY

I COULD BE KING OF THE JUNGLE
www.garfield.com Distributed by Universal Press Syndicate
IF I WANTED TO BE
© 2002 PAWS, INC. All Rights Reserved.
AND IF THE JUNGLE HAD AIR CONDITIONING
JIM DAVIS 8-3

GARFIELD®
YOU CAN TELL A LOT ABOUT A MOUSE BY HIS MOUSEHOLE
www.garfield.com
FAT MOUSE...
SKINNY MOUSE...
© 2002 PAWS, INC. All Rights Reserved.
TALL MOUSE...
Distributed by Universal Press Syndicate
HOWDY!
AH
JIM DAVIS 8-4

DOES YOUR LITTLE BUDDY THERE WANT TO ORDER FROM THE CHILDREN'S MENU?
JIM DAVIS 8-5
© 2002 PAWS, INC. All Rights Reserved.
www.garfield.com
Distributed by Universal Press Syndicate
AND WHEN I **TRY** TO BE FUNNY...
WAH-HA-HA-HA-HA-HA!!

YOU CHANGED YOUR MENU!
YEAH
JIM DAVIS 8-6
© 2002 PAWS, INC. All Rights Reserved.
CHEF TONY IS EXPERIMENTING WITH MORE EXOTIC FARE
www.garfield.com
Distributed by Universal Press Syndicate
"AARDVARK TARTARE"?
ENOUGH KETCHUP AND IT ALL TASTES THE SAME!

WHAT COMES WITH THE DINNER?
BREAD AND YOUR CHOICE OF POTATO
JIM DAVIS 8-7
© 2002 PAWS, INC. All Rights Reserved.
WHAT ARE MY CHOICES?
www.garfield.com
Distributed by Universal Press Syndicate
COOKED OR RAW
THE RITZ, THIS AIN'T

I'LL HAVE THE CHILI
JIM DAVIS 8-8
www.garfield.com
Distributed by Universal Press Syndicate
SURE THING, HON
© 2002 PAWS, INC. All Rights Reserved.
SIGN THIS RELEASE FORM
DINER CHILI... GOTTA LOVE IT

IRMA! WHAT HAPPENED TO YOUR FINGER?
www.garfield.com
Distributed by Universal Press Syndicate
I BURNED IT IN THE KITCHEN WHILE PREPARING **YOUR** FOOD!
JIM DAVIS 8-9
© 2002 PAWS, INC. All Rights Reserved.
HOW CAN I EAT WHEN I'M CONSUMED WITH GUILT?
HERE, (BURP) I'LL SHOW YOU

I'D LIKE THE "WHOOP-DEE-DOO" BURGER
JIM DAVIS 8-10
Menu
Distributed by Universal Press Syndicate
FRIES OR SLAW?
FRIES
www.garfield.com
© 2002 PAWS, INC. All Rights Reserved.
CONFETTI OR STREAMERS?
CONFETTI!
IS THE CLOWN EXTRA?

Garfield
www.garfield.com
© 2002 PAWS, INC. All Rights Reserved.
Distributed by Universal Press Syndicate
GARFIELD!
JIM DAVIS 8·11
YOU'RE LETTING THE COLD AIR OUT!
HEL-LOOOOO!

MMMM MMM
I LOVE ME
JIM DAVIS 8·12
Distributed by Universal Press Syndicate
© 2002 PAWS, INC. All Rights Reserved.
www.garfield.com

I SEE YOU TWO HAVE FINALLY MADE UP
YEP
IT'S STUPID TO FIGHT OVER SOMETHING AS SILLY AS EACH OTHER'S FOOD!
WE AGREE
THAT'S WHY WE DECIDED TO EAT YOURS INSTEAD
HEY!
JIM DAVIS 8·13
Distributed by Universal Press Syndicate
© 2002 PAWS, INC. All Rights Reserved.
www.garfield.com

JIM DAVIS 8·14
IS IT TRUE YOU YELL AT ANIMALS?
GO AWAY!
A SHOCKING ADMISSION!
Distributed by Universal Press Syndicate
© 2002 PAWS, INC. All Rights Reserved.
www.garfield.com

GARFIELD, YOU HAVE TO GET UP
IF YOU WANT TO EAT, YOU HAVE TO GO INTO THE KITCHEN
WILL THERE BE ANY HILLS?
JIM DAVIS 8-15
Distributed by Universal Press Syndicate
© 2002 PAWS, INC. All Rights Reserved.
www.garfield.com

SQUEEK
SQUEEK
SQUEEK
SQUEE
I'M ON, AREN'T I?
JIM DAVIS 8-16
Distributed by Universal Press Syndicate
© 2002 PAWS, INC. All Rights Reserved.
www.garfield.com

JON GAVE ME THIS BALL OF YARN FOR MY BIRTHDAY
SOME ASSEMBLY REQUIRED
JIM DAVIS 8-17
Distributed by Universal Press Syndicate
© 2002 PAWS, INC. All Rights Reserved.
www.garfield.com

Garfield®
TODAY WE WILL DISCUSS...
THE HUMAN:
HIS FOIBLES...
...HIS INSECURITIES...
...HIS BACON...
TOUCH IT AND I'LL TIE YOUR THUMBS IN A KNOT!
JIM DAVIS 8-18
Distributed by Universal Press Syndicate
www.garfield.com
© 2002 PAWS, INC. All Rights Reserved.

I REALLY SHOULD GET UP
Distributed by Universal Press Syndicate
www.garfield.com
© 2002 PAWS, INC. All Rights Reserved.
YOU REALLY SHOULD GET UP
BEEN THERE. TRIED THAT. DIDN'T WORK
JIM DAVIS 8-19

YOU KNOW, YOU'RE NOT VERY THRILLING
Distributed by Universal Press Syndicate
www.garfield.com
© 2002 PAWS, INC. All Rights Reserved.
STOP STEALING MY LINES
JIM DAVIS 8-20

LOOK AT THAT POOR CAT, MARTHA
JIM DAVIS 8-21
© 2002 PAWS, INC. All Rights Reserved.
WELL, DEAR, HE'S IN KITTY HEAVEN NOW
www.garfield.com
Distributed by Universal Press Syndicate
WHY DON'T YOU GO GET A SHOVEL?
MAYBE I SHOULD MOVE SOMETHING

YES, I SENSE A PRESENCE...
JIM DAVIS 8-22
© 2002 PAWS, INC. All Rights Reserved.
I HEAR MOURNFUL CRIES
www.garfield.com
Distributed by Universal Press Syndicate
YES, IT'S THE RESTLESS SOULS OF A THOUSAND DONUTS
GO AWAY

WHAT A WASTE!
© 2002 PAWS, INC. All Rights Reserved.
ANOTHER DAY HAS PASSED YOU BY, GARFIELD
www.garfield.com
Distributed by Universal Press Syndicate
YOU DON'T HAVE THAT MANY LEFT!
AND YOU'D THINK I COULD SPEND THEM IN PEACE!
JIM DAVIS 8-23

YOU JUST DON'T CARE ABOUT ANYTHING, DO YOU?!
JIM DAVIS 8-24
© 2002 PAWS, INC. All Rights Reserved.
WHY, AT THIS VERY MINUTE A METEOR COULD BE HURTLING TOWARD THIS VERY SPOT!
Distributed by Universal Press Syndicate
www.garfield.com

GARFIELD
GEEZ IT'S A SCORCHER!
NOT EVEN ELEVEN O'CLOCK AND IT'S SWELTERING!
I'M MELTING! HOW IS ANY LIVING THING SUPPOSED TO STAND THIS?!
'MORNING, SLEEPYHEAD. HERE'S YOUR COFFEE
SLUP
THIS IS COLD!!!
JIM DAVIS 8-25

HOW CAN YOU NOT LOVE CATS?
YOU ANNOY ME
I WASN'T TALKING TO YOU, BUSTER
© 2002 PAWS, INC. All Rights Reserved.
www.garfield.com Distributed by Universal Press Syndicate
JIM DAVIS 8-26

SNIFF SNIFF
NO...
JIM DAVIS 8-27 © 2002 PAWS, INC. All Rights Reserved.
SNI-
AH!
Distributed by Universal Press Syndicate www.garfield.com
-JUST TRY AND BEAT A SUMMER AFTERNOON DOWNWIND OF A BARBECUE!

I NOW REALIZE WHY I EAT SO MUCH
© 2002 PAWS, INC. All Rights Reserved.
I SUFFER FROM LOW SELF-ESTEEM
Distributed by Universal Press Syndicate www.garfield.com
YOU'RE A FAT SLOB
AND YOU'RE HELPING
JIM DAVIS 8-28

COACH WAS VERY CRITICAL OF MY PLAYING
I REMEMBER ONE GAME IN PARTICULAR...
HE RAN INTO THE STANDS AND SLAPPED MY PARENTS
THEY MUST HAVE BEEN SO PROUD
JIM DAVIS 8-29
www.garfield.com
Distributed by Universal Press Syndicate
© 2002 PAWS, INC. All Rights Reserved.

YOU'D MISS ME IF I STOPPED CALLING, ELLEN
NO, I DON'T WANT TO TEST THAT THEORY
AND NO, NOT FOR TEN DOLLARS
DO I HEAR TWENTY?
JIM DAVIS 8-30
© 2002 PAWS, INC. All Rights Reserved.
Distributed by Universal Press Syndicate
www.garfield.com

I DON'T HAVE ANY ROLE MODELS...
NO ONE TO LOOK UP TO...
HOWEVER, THERE ARE THOSE I CAN LOOK DOWN ON
JIM DAVIS 8-31
© 2002 PAWS, INC. All Rights Reserved.
www.garfield.com
Distributed by Universal Press Syndicate

GARFIELD
HELLO, EVELYN? THIS IS JON ARBUCKLE
WOULD YOU CARE TO JOIN ME IN A LITTLE FINE DINING THIS EVENING?
I KNOW THIS COZY LITTLE OUT-OF-THE-WAY SEAFOOD BISTRO...
WONDERFUL FOOD... GREAT ATMOSPHERE...
PARDON?
STINKY BOB'S SUSHI BAR AND BAIT SHACK
CUE THE CRUSHING REJECTION
JIM DAVIS 9.1
www.garfield.com
© 2002 PAWS, INC. All Rights Reserved.
Distributed by Universal Press Syndicate

CATCH THAT MOUSE!
© 2002 PAWS, INC. All Rights Reserved.
OKAY
HANG ON. LET ME GO SLIP ON MY RUNNING SHOES
JIM DAVIS 9-2
Distributed by Universal Press Syndicate www.garfield.com
SEEMS LIKE A REASONABLE REQUEST

© 2002 PAWS, INC. All Rights Reserved.
ANY LUCK?
JIM DAVIS 9-3
SOME
www.garfield.com Distributed by Universal Press Syndicate
I GOT THE POTATO CHIP, BUT THE DIP IS JUST OUT OF REACH

AHEM...
JIM DAVIS 9-4
© 2002 PAWS, INC. All Rights Reserved.
I WOULD LIKE TO THANK EVERYONE WHO MADE MY MOUSE-OF-THE-YEAR AWARD POSSIBLE
www.garfield.com Distributed by Universal Press Syndicate
OH, GARFIELD...
CAN'T YOU SEE I'M BUSY WATCHING THE MOUSE-HOLE?

GARFIELD, WHY DON'T YOU CATCH MICE?
ARE YOU AFRAID OF THEM?
JIM DAVIS 9-5
WHAT POWER DO THEY HAVE OVER YOU?
TINY LITTLE INCRIMINATING PHOTOGRAPHS
© 2002 PAWS, INC. All Rights Reserved.
Distributed by Universal Press Syndicate
www.garfield.com

HELLO, PEST CONTROL?
THERE'S A HUGE RAT IN MY TRASH
JIM DAVIS 9-6
I **HAVE** A CAT!
YOU **HAD** A CAT
© 2002 PAWS, INC. All Rights Reserved.
Distributed by Universal Press Syndicate
www.garfield.com

...AND THEN THE GIANT MOUSE CHASED THE EVIL CAT AWAY
BEDTIME Stories
EVERYONE ATE CHEESE AND LIVED HAPPILY EVER AFTER. THE END
THAT WAS AN ODD ONE
EXCUSE ME. WHO SAID YOU COULD BORROW THAT?
JIM DAVIS 9-7
www.garfield.com
© 2002 PAWS, INC. All Rights Reserved.
Distributed by Universal Press Syndicate

GARFIELD
WAIT HERE, GARFIELD. I'VE GOT TO WORK OUT
GYM
www.garfield.com
HUUUUP!
JUICE BAR
EEEYYYAHH
SAUNA
Distributed by Universal Press Syndicate
EEEERRGGGHHH
VENDING MACHINE
JIM DAVIS 9-8
OOO! OOO! OOO! OOO! OOO!
HOT TUB
© 2002 PAWS, INC. All Rights Reserved.
LET'S GO GET SOME ICE CREAM
GYM
COOL DOWN

JIM DAVIS 9-9
www.garfield.com
Distributed by Universal Press Syndicate
SHHHH
© 2002 PAWS, INC. All Rights Reserved.
STALKING THE WILD PIZZA

YOU TWO SHOULD STOP BEING SO COMPETITIVE
www.garfield.com
Distributed by Universal Press Syndicate
OKAY, JON, WE WILL
© 2002 PAWS, INC. All Rights Reserved.
BUT SINCE YOU BROUGHT THE SUBJECT UP, WHICH ONE OF US WOULD YOU SAY WAS MORE COMPETITIVE?
JIM DAVIS 9-10

JIM DAVIS 9-11
YOU KNOW, GARFIELD...
www.garfield.com
Distributed by Universal Press Syndicate
LIFE IS STRANGE
© 2002 PAWS, INC. All Rights Reserved.
SO IS YOUR SHIRT, BUT YOU DON'T HEAR ME BLAMING LIFE FOR IT

GARFIELD, WOULD YOU MISS ME IF I WENT AWAY?
HMMM...
IT'S A DEAL!
www.garfield.com
Distributed by Universal Press Syndicate
© 2002 PAWS, INC. All Rights Reserved.
JIM DAVIS 9-12

ONCE YOU THINK YOU'VE REACHED THE PINNACLE OF BOREDOM...
17,887... 17,888... 17,889...
17,890 ARM HAIRS!
...THE BAR IS RAISED ONCE AGAIN
ONE...TWO... THREE...
www.garfield.com
Distributed by Universal Press Syndicate
© 2002 PAWS, INC. All Rights Reserved.
JIM DAVIS 9-13

OOPS, MY PANTS ARE ON BACKWARDS
ARE YOU SURE IT ISN'T YOU WHO'S BACKWARDS?
BECAUSE FRANKLY, YOUR PANTS LOOK SMARTER THAN YOU
www.garfield.com
Distributed by Universal Press Syndicate
© 2002 PAWS, INC. All Rights Reserved.
JIM DAVIS 9-14

GARFIELD
SIR, THIS IS THE 12-ITEM EXPRESS LANE AND YOU HAVE 13
TRUDY
COME ON...IT'S JUST ONE MORE ITEM
RULES ARE RULES
GULP
THERE... TWELVE
GRAB
SWISH
*BEEP*
KA-CHING!
I DIDN'T KNOW YOU HAD A BAR CODE
JUST KEEP PUSHING
JIM DAVIS 9-15
Distributed by Universal Press Syndicate
© 2002 PAWS, INC. All Rights Reserved.
www.garfield.com

STAY TUNED FOR A RECITATION OF THE COMPLETE WORKS OF SHAKESPEARE
JIM DAVIS 9-16
www.garfield.com
Distributed by Universal Press Syndicate
SOUNDS GOOD
© 2002 PAWS, INC. All Rights Reserved.
I LOST THE REMOTE

WE'RE TALKING TO HOG FARMER EARL DUROC...
© 2002 PAWS, INC. All Rights Reserved.
JIM DAVIS 9-17
TELL ME, EARL, DO THEY LIKE BEING BURIED IN THE DIRT LIKE THAT?
www.garfield.com
Distributed by Universal Press Syndicate
OH YEAH, YOU WATER 'EM AND THEY GROW REAL BIG
YOU GOT HIM HOOKED, EARL, NOW REEL HIM IN

THE ACTION CHANNEL PRESENTS...
www.garfield.com
Distributed by Universal Press Syndicate
THE ADVENTURES OF MARK VENEER...
© 2002 PAWS, INC. All Rights Reserved.
JIM DAVIS 9-18
THE CRIME-FIGHTING MIME!
WRITERS' STRIKE

AND THE WINNER OF THE UGLY BABY PAGEANT IS...
LITTLE ROBERTA SACONSKI!
NO PICTURES... PLEEEASE
I DOUBT IF LITTLE ROBERTA WILL BE ASKED TO THE PROM
www.garfield.com Distributed by Universal Press Syndicate
© 2002 PAWS, INC. All Rights Reserved.
JPM DAVPS 9-19

WE CLOWNS LAUGH ON THE OUTSIDE
AND CRY ON THE INSIDE
HOW FASCINATING, BINKY. TELL US MORE
I'M AWAKE ON THE OUTSIDE AND ASLEEP ON THE INSIDE
www.garfield.com Distributed by Universal Press Syndicate
© 2002 PAWS, INC. All Rights Reserved.
JPM DAVPS 9-20

THE CATERPILLAR IS EMERGING FROM THE COCOON TO BECOME...
A RARE AMAZONIAN VAMPIRE MOTH!
NECK! IT'S ON MY NECK!
SOMETIMES YOU CAN'T IMPROVE UPON REAL LIFE
www.garfield.com Distributed by Universal Press Syndicate
© 2002 PAWS, INC. All Rights Reserved.
JPM DAVPS 9-21

GARFIELD
WELL, THIS IS A NICE BLIND DATE
IT SURE IS
JIM DAVIS 9-22
www.garfield.com
YOU'RE JON, RIGHT?
YES... AND WHAT IS YOUR NAME AGAIN?
EUPHEMIA
MMMPH!
Distributed by Universal Press Syndicate
DO YOU FIND MY NAME AMUSING?
NOPE!... JUST A LITTLE LEG CRAMP...
THAT'S A FUNNY EXPRESSION FOR A LEG CRAMP
I'M... LAUGHING THROUGH THE PAIN... EEEEEEE-
© 2002 PAWS, INC. All Rights Reserved.
-EEEEUPHEMIA!! HAW! HAW! HAW! HAW! HAW!
SNORT! SNORT!
DIDN'T EVEN MAKE IT PAST THE BREADSTICKS

WOULD YOU DO ME A FAVOR?
Distributed by Universal Press Syndicate www.garfield.com
ABSOLUTELY!
© 2002 PAWS, INC. All Rights Reserved.
EVENTUALLY. PROBABLY BY ACCIDENT. BUT IT COULD HAPPEN
NEVER MIND
JIM DAVIS 9-23

I GOTTA DANCE!
Distributed by Universal Press Syndicate www.garfield.com
OW!
© 2002 PAWS, INC. All Rights Reserved.
I GOTTA CALL AN AMBULANCE!
MY KNEE!
JIM DAVIS 9-24

ANYTHING HAPPEN AROUND HERE TODAY?
Distributed by Universal Press Syndicate www.garfield.com
WELL, ASIDE FROM YOU ASKING ME IF ANYTHING HAPPENED AROUND HERE TODAY...
© 2002 PAWS, INC. All Rights Reserved.
NOTHING
JIM DAVIS 9-25

I AM SO BORED
I'M DRAWING FACES ON ALL THE PILLOWS!
AND JON IS SO LONELY
JIM DAVIS 9-26
www.garfield.com
Distributed by Universal Press Syndicate
© 2002 PAWS, INC. All Rights Reserved.

MY DATE INSISTED WE SIT AT SEPARATE TABLES AT THE RESTAURANT
SHE SAID I LOOK BETTER FROM A DISTANCE
DO YOU THINK I LOOK BETTER FROM A DISTANCE?
NO, JUST MORE GULLIBLE
JIM DAVIS 9-27
www.garfield.com
Distributed by Universal Press Syndicate
© 2002 PAWS, INC. All Rights Reserved.

THIS ISN'T REAL
HOW ABOUT THAT...
A FAKE HEAD!
JIM DAVIS 9-28
www.garfield.com
Distributed by Universal Press Syndicate
© 2002 PAWS, INC. All Rights Reserved.

GARFIELD
GAR-FIELD!
PRESENT
DID YOU DO THAT?!!
HMM...LET'S SEE... CALLOUS DISRESPECT FOR PERSONAL PROPERTY...
...UTTER DESTRUCTION ON A SCALE INCOMPREHENSIBLE TO THE CIVILIZED MIND...
AND CAT HAIR EVERYWHERE
NOPE
JIM DAVIS 9-29

I'M GOING TO HAVE TO GET UP
Distributed by Universal Press Syndicate www.garfield.com
NO, WAIT
© 2002 PAWS, INC. All Rights Reserved.
I JUST GOT MY SECOND WIND
JIM DAVIS 9-30

TIME TO WATER THE PLANTS
Distributed by Universal Press Syndicate www.garfield.com
© 2002 PAWS, INC. All Rights Reserved.
SUBTLETY, THY NAME IS **NOT** JON
JIM DAVIS 10-1

ODIE, YOUR TAIL SAYS YOU'RE A NOODLE-NECK STUPID HEAD
JIM DAVIS 10-2
Distributed by Universal Press Syndicate www.garfield.com
ARE YOU GOING TO TAKE THAT?
© 2002 PAWS, INC. All Rights Reserved.
I WONDER WHY DOGS CHASE THEIR TAILS
YIP! YIP! YIP!
IT'S A MYSTERY!

www.garfield.com
Distributed by Universal Press Syndicate
ODIE HAS A GIRLFRIEND!
© 2002 PAWS, INC. All Rights Reserved.
PLEASE DON'T LET THEM MULTIPLY!
JIM DAVIS 10-3

I'VE GOTTA GET OUT OF HERE!
JIM DAVIS 10-4
www.garfield.com
Distributed by Universal Press Syndicate
THERE MUST BE SOMEPLACE TO HIDE!
© 2002 PAWS, INC. All Rights Reserved.
WHO WANTS TO HELP ME LOOK FOR CORNFLAKES THAT LOOK LIKE CELEBRITIES?
TOO LATE!
CORN FLAKES

HAVE A BOWL OF ROCKS, ODIE!
ODIE
www.garfield.com
Distributed by Universal Press Syndicate
CRUNCH CRUNCH CRUNCH CRUNCH
JIM DAVIS 10-5
© 2002 PAWS, INC. All Rights Reserved.
CRUNCH CRUNCH CRUNCH CRUNCH
THAT SOUNDS KINDA GOOD
DIE

GARFIELD®
WHY DON'T YOU EVER LISTEN TO ME?
HUH?
WHY DON'T YOU EVER AGREE WITH ME?
THAT'S NOT TRUE
WHY DON'T YOU SHOW ME ANY RESPECT?
I DO... BONEHEAD
WHY DON'T YOU EVER SHOW AFFECTION?
CATCH ME AROUND A MIRROR SOMETIME
WHY DO YOU CAUSE ME SO MUCH GRIEF?!
BECAUSE I'M A CAT
AND WHY DO I STILL LOVE YOU ANYWAY?
SEE PREVIOUS ANSWER
JIM DAVIS 10-6
www.garfield.com
Distributed by Universal Press Syndicate
© 2002 PAWS, INC. All Rights Reserved.

I COULDN'T DECIDE WHICH SHIRT TO WEAR...
www.garfield.com
Distributed by Universal Press Syndicate
SO I PUT ALL OF THEM ON
© 2002 PAWS, INC. All Rights Reserved.
I COULDN'T DECIDE WHAT TO EAT, SO I ATE EVERYTHING!
WHERE'S THE REFRIGERATOR?
JIM DAVIS 10-7

WHAT DO YOU WANT FOR DINNER?
www.garfield.com
Distributed by Universal Press Syndicate
WHO ARE YOU TALKING TO?
JIM DAVIS 10-8
© 2002 PAWS, INC. All Rights Reserved.
I MEAN, IS THERE ANYTHING YOU DON'T WANT?
RAISINS

NATURE HOLDS MANY DANGERS
www.garfield.com
Distributed by Universal Press Syndicate
SQUIRRELS WITH MINIATURE WEED WHACKERS!
© 2002 PAWS, INC. All Rights Reserved.
ESPECIALLY THESE DAYS
JIM DAVIS 10-9

THIS IS ALL I'LL BE SHEDDING TODAY
I DREAD TOMORROW
JIM DAVIS 10-10

I COULD BE ON A DATE NOW
BUT I CHOOSE TO JUST SIT HERE WITH YOU
THE THINGS I DO FOR THE WOMEN OF THE WORLD
JIM DAVIS 10-11

JIM DAVIS 10-12
STAY IN CHARACTER, GARFIELD

GARFIELD
HELLO!
I'M LOOKING FOR A MASSEUR!
...ONE WHO CAN DELIVER A VIGOROUS DEEP-TISSUE MASSAGE! CAN YOU RECOMMEND ANYONE?
WHOMP!
DO YOU HAVE A CARD?
JIM DAVIS 10.13
Distributed by Universal Press Syndicate
www.garfield.com
© 2002 PAWS, INC. All Rights Reserved.

HOW ARE YOU, JON?
I HAVE A HEADACHE
AS IF YOU CARE
GOOD TO HEAR. HAVE A NICE DAY
JIM DAVIS 10-14
Distributed by Universal Press Syndicate www.garfield.com
© 2002 PAWS, INC. All Rights Reserved.

YAAAAH!
OKAY, GARFIELD! STAY CALM!
WAY AHEAD OF YOU
JIM DAVIS 10-15
Distributed by Universal Press Syndicate www.garfield.com
© 2002 PAWS, INC. All Rights Reserved.

AAAAHHH!
YAAAAAHHH!
AREN'T YOU CURIOUS TO KNOW WHAT THAT WAS ABOUT?
NOT UNLESS IT WILL CAUSE DINNER TO BE LATE
JIM DAVIS 10-16
Distributed by Universal Press Syndicate www.garfield.com
© 2002 PAWS, INC. All Rights Reserved.

I HAD A PRETTY GOOD DAY TODAY
THREE... TWO... ONE...
ONCE I GOT MY LEG OUT OF THAT BEAR TRAP
JON NEVER DISAPPOINTS ME
JIM DAVIS 10-17
www.garfield.com
Distributed by Universal Press Syndicate
© 2002 PAWS, INC. All Rights Reserved.

SOMETIMES I FEEL LIKE A FAILURE
OH, COME ON, JON!
SOMETIMES?!
JIM DAVIS 10-18
www.garfield.com
Distributed by Universal Press Syndicate
© 2002 PAWS, INC. All Rights Reserved.

BOY, THE SUN SURE SET EARLY TODAY
BURNED-OUT LIGHT BULB
OKAY, SO I'M NO NATURE EXPERT
JIM DAVIS 10-19
www.garfield.com
Distributed by Universal Press Syndicate
© 2002 PAWS, INC. All Rights Reserved.

GARFIELD
AH, AUTUMN. WHEN MOTHER NATURE EXPRESSES HERSELF,
PAINTING FROM A PALETTE SO RICH AND SO FULL.
THE EYES DO DANCE WITH DELIGHT,
AND DRINK DEEPLY FROM THIS, THE SWEETEST SEASON OF ALL.
VOOOOO
I SINCERELY DOUBT THAT POETS HAVE PENNED ANY LOVING ODES TO LEAF BLOWERS
JPM DAVIS 10-20
Distributed by Universal Press Syndicate
www.garfield.com
© 2002 PAWS, INC. All Rights Reserved.

Z
JIM DAVIS 10-21
Distributed by Universal Press Syndicate
www.garfield.com
GO BACK TO SLEEP
© 2002 PAWS, INC. All Rights Reserved.
HEY, DON'T KNOCK IT. I'VE LASTED LONGER THAN ANY CLOCK AROUND HERE
Z

I'M GOING OUTSIDE FOR AWHILE
Distributed by Universal Press Syndicate
www.garfield.com
JIM DAVIS 10-22
© 2002 PAWS, INC. All Rights Reserved.
BRR...IT'S COLD OUT THERE
YOU WERE IN THE REFRIGERATOR!

SOCK PUPPET IMPRESSION
Distributed by Universal Press Syndicate
www.garfield.com
© 2002 PAWS, INC. All Rights Reserved.
THE INVISIBLE MAN!
GO AWAY
JIM DAVIS 10-23

JIM DAVIS 10-24
I'M THE WORLD'S FASTEST SPIDER!
ZIP
www.garfield.com
Distributed by Universal Press Syndicate
SCHWOP
© 2002 PAWS, INC. All Rights Reserved.
OKAY, OKAY, SECOND FASTEST

I AM A TINY SPIDER!
www.garfield.com
Distributed by Universal Press Syndicate
SWAT
© 2002 PAWS, INC. All Rights Reserved.
AND THIS IS A TINY MAGAZINE!
JIM DAVIS 10-25

REMEMBER THAT TIME I CHASED YOU?
JIM DAVIS 10-26
www.garfield.com
Distributed by Universal Press Syndicate
AND YOU FELL INTO A PIT FULL OF ANGRY MONKEYS?
© 2002 PAWS, INC. All Rights Reserved.
NOW THAT WAS FUNNY!
THIS IS WHY NONE OF THE GREAT COMEDIANS ARE DOGS

GARFIELD
PLOP!
EXCUSE ME, MISTER...
I'M A POOR, DEFENSELESS LITTLE BABY BIRD WHO JUST FELL OUT OF HIS NEST...
COULD YOU HELP ME BACK UP THERE SO I CAN BE WITH ALLLLLLLLLLLL MY BROTHERS AND SISTERS AGAIN?
OH, STOP WITH ALL THE DISAPPROVING GLARES ALREADY
JIM DAVIS 10-27
Distributed by Universal Press Syndicate
www.garfield.com
© 2002 PAWS, INC. All Rights Reserved.

I AM GOING TO FOLLOW MY DREAMS, GARFIELD
JIM DAVIS 10-28
www.garfield.com
Distributed by Universal Press Syndicate
YOU DON'T HAVE ANY DREAMS, DO YOU?
© 2002 PAWS, INC. All Rights Reserved.
ASIDE FROM THE DANCING MONKEY IN THE CHOCOLATE FONDUE POT, NO

I WAS MUCH MORE ACTIVE THAN YOU TODAY
www.garfield.com
Distributed by Universal Press Syndicate
I WOULD HAVE BEEN ACTIVE TOO...
© 2002 PAWS, INC. All Rights Reserved.
JIM DAVIS 10-29
IF I'D CAUGHT **MY** TIE IN THE BLENDER!

...AND THAT'S WHAT I DID TODAY!
www.garfield.com
Distributed by Universal Press Syndicate
HOW ABOUT YOU?
© 2002 PAWS, INC. All Rights Reserved.
I SPENT THE DAY LISTENING TO WHAT YOU DID TODAY
JIM DAVIS 10-30

I CARRY A PICTURE OF YOU IN MY WALLET
REALLY?
I SHOW IT TO LOTS OF PEOPLE
ALL RIGHT!
IT GETS ME LOTS OF SYMPATHY
YOU SNUCK UP ON ME WITH THAT ONE!
JIM DAVIS 10-31
www.garfield.com
Distributed by Universal Press Syndicate
© 2002 PAWS, INC. All Rights Reserved.

ON THE FARM, WE WERE CLOSE TO NATURE, GARFIELD
JIM DAVIS 11-1
I REMEMBER RUNNING BAREFOOT THROUGH THE COW PASTURE
BOY, WAS THAT DISGUSTING
YOU MAY STOP RIGHT THERE
www.garfield.com
Distributed by Universal Press Syndicate
© 2002 PAWS, INC. All Rights Reserved.

IS IT MY IMAGINATION, OR DO YOU INSULT ME AT EVERY OPPORTUNITY?
THAT'S ASSUMING YOU **HAVE** AN IMAGINATION
JIM DAVIS 11-2
www.garfield.com
Distributed by Universal Press Syndicate
© 2002 PAWS, INC. All Rights Reserved.

GARFIELD
www.garfield.com
© 2002 PAWS, INC. All Rights Reserved.
Distributed by Universal Press Syndicate
SMACK
SMACK
SMACK
ALL RIGHT, I'LL TURN THE FURNACE ON!
JIM DAVIS 11-3

RUN! IT'S THE CAT!
www.garfield.com
Distributed by Universal Press Syndicate
WE CAN'T RUN, YOU IDIOT! WE'RE PLANTS!
© 2002 PAWS, INC. All Rights Reserved.
JIM DAVIS 11-4
I SENSE FEAR
THEN TIP OVER AND ROLL!

JIM DAVIS 11-5
www.garfield.com
Distributed by Universal Press Syndicate
© 2002 PAWS, INC. All Rights Reserved.
YOU MADE LEMONADE
I GOTTA START READING INSTRUCTIONS

JIM DAVIS 11-6
www.garfield.com
Distributed by Universal Press Syndicate
© 2002 PAWS, INC. All Rights Reserved.
TOOK MY BALL OF YARN FOR A WALK

AH, NATURE!
DID YOU FORGET TO PAY THE NATURE BILL?
JIM DAVIS 11-7
Distributed by Universal Press Syndicate www.garfield.com
© 2002 PAWS, INC. All Rights Reserved.

JIM DAVIS 11-8
MEOW!
MEOW!
THAT WOULD BE FOR ME
Distributed by Universal Press Syndicate www.garfield.com
© 2002 PAWS, INC. All Rights Reserved.

JIM DAVIS 11-9
MY FOOT'S ASLEEP
AND DREAMING
Distributed by Universal Press Syndicate www.garfield.com
© 2002 PAWS, INC. All Rights Reserved.

GARFIELD®
DOG TREATS
YOU HAVE THAT LOOK IN YOUR EYE...
THAT LOOK THAT SAYS YOU'RE GOING TO EXPRESS MAIL THE DOG TO A FOREIGN EMBASSY...
THAT SAYS YOU'RE GOING TO LACE MY UNDERWEAR DRAWER WITH ITCHING POWDER...
THAT SAYS YOU'RE GOING TO PERFORM A HORRIBLE PRACTICAL JOKE ON ME WHILE I'M ASLEEP. I KNOW THAT LOOK
BY THE WAY, HAVE YOU SEEN ODIE?
SCRATCH SCRATCH SCRATCH
I GOTTA GET A NEW LOOK
JPM DAVPS 11-10

I'M GOING TO GNAW ON THE WOODWORK
I HOPE YOU GET A SPLINTER!
JIM DAVIS 11-11
www.garfield.com
Distributed by Universal Press Syndicate
© 2002 PAWS, INC. All Rights Reserved.

FILTHY VERMIN!
YEAH!
IT WOULDN'T HURT YOU TO TAKE A SHOWER!
JIM DAVIS 11-12
www.garfield.com
Distributed by Universal Press Syndicate
© 2002 PAWS, INC. All Rights Reserved.

WHY AREN'T YOU CHASING THE MOUSE?
THE MOUSE?
OH, I DIDN'T RECOGNIZE HIM IN THOSE GLASSES
JIM DAVIS 11-13
www.garfield.com
Distributed by Universal Press Syndicate
© 2002 PAWS, INC. All Rights Reserved.

GARFIELD, WHAT'S THAT NOISE?
UH...WHAT NOISE?
SQUEEK
SQUEEK
SQUEEK
www.garfield.com
Distributed by Universal Press Syndicate
SOUNDS LIKE MICE
I'M BABYSITTING
SQUEEK
SQUEEK
SQUEEK
© 2002 PAWS, INC. All Rights Reserved.
TELL ME IT'S NOT
THEY'RE GIVING ME CHEESE
SQUEEK
SQUEE
SQUEEK
JIM DAVIS 11-14

HEY!
www.garfield.com
Distributed by Universal Press Syndicate
PICK IT UP!
© 2002 PAWS, INC. All Rights Reserved.
I ALMOST CAUGHT YOU!
SORRY
JIM DAVIS 11-15

I GUESS A HOUSE WITH A FAT CAT SHOULD HAVE A FAT MOUSE, TOO
JIM DAVIS 11-16
www.garfield.com
Distributed by Universal Press Syndicate
WHAT ARE YOU TALKING ABOUT?
© 2002 PAWS, INC. All Rights Reserved.
I AM NOT FAT! I'M JUST BIG BONED

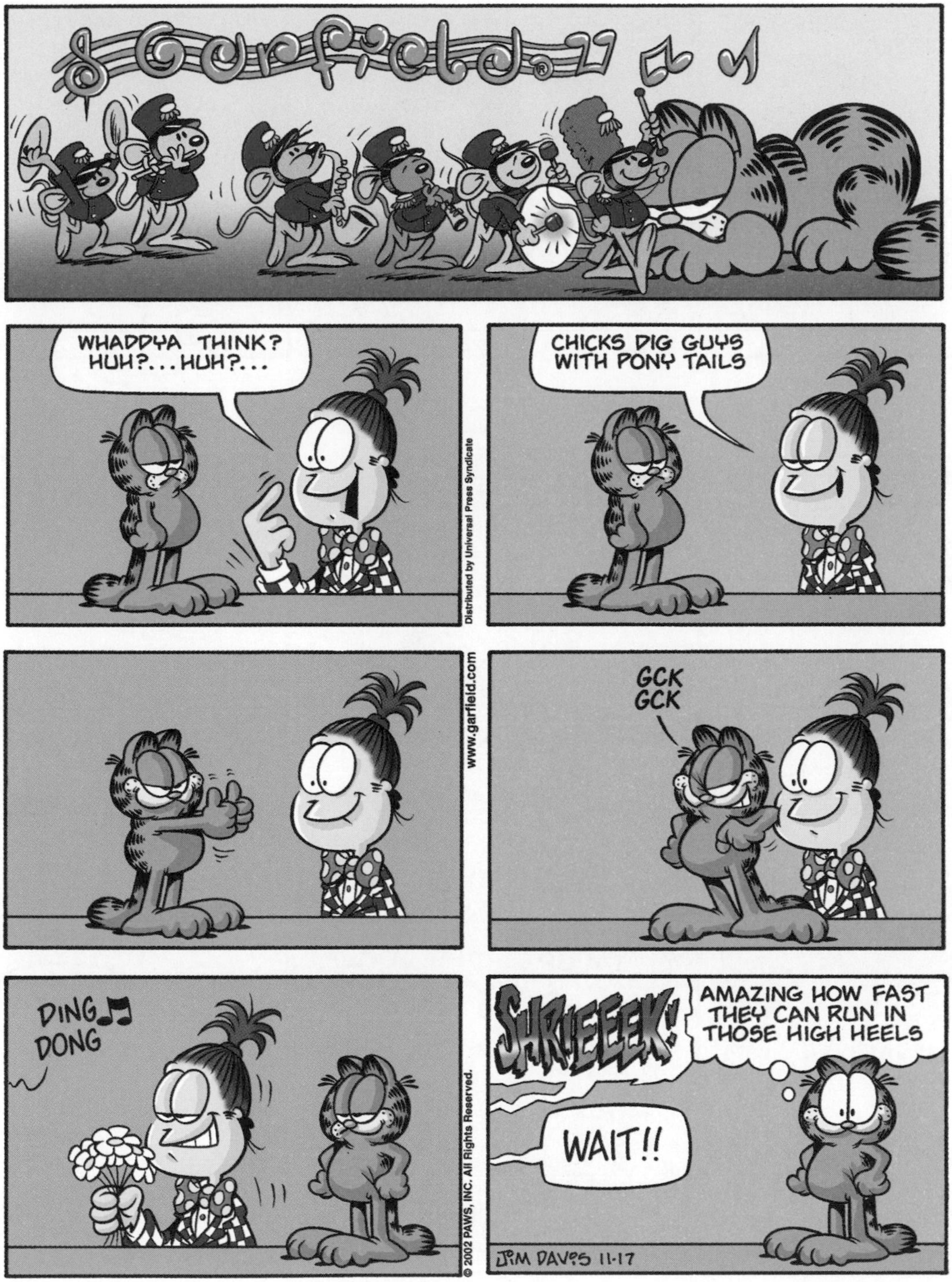
Garfield®
WHADDYA THINK? HUH?... HUH?...
CHICKS DIG GUYS WITH PONY TAILS
GCK GCK
DING DONG
SHRIEEEK!
AMAZING HOW FAST THEY CAN RUN IN THOSE HIGH HEELS
WAIT!!
JIM DAVIS 11-17
Distributed by Universal Press Syndicate
www.garfield.com
© 2002 PAWS, INC. All Rights Reserved.

IT'S SOCKO THE SUPERHERO SOCK PUPPET!
www.garfield.com
Distributed by Universal Press Syndicate
AND HIS TRUSTY SIDEKICK, FUZZY SLIPPER MAN!
© 2002 PAWS, INC. All Rights Reserved.
THERE'S SOMETHING WRONG WITH THAT MAN
YOU SAID IT
JIM DAVIS 11-18

MY LIFE IS WITHOUT MEANING!
www.garfield.com
Distributed by Universal Press Syndicate
BAT
© 2002 PAWS, INC. All Rights Reserved.
I TAKE IT ALL BACK!
JIM DAVIS 11-19

RIIINNNNNG!
www.garfield.com
Distributed by Universal Press Syndicate
ALL RIGHT. I'M UP
JUST DOING MY JOB
© 2002 PAWS, INC. All Rights Reserved.
Z
JIM DAVIS 11-20

YOU'RE STANDING IN MY FOOD!
JIM DAVIS 11-21
www.garfield.com
Distributed by Universal Press Syndicate
SORRY
© 2002 PAWS, INC. All Rights Reserved.

YOU ONLY DATE ATHLETIC TYPES?
JIM DAVIS 11-22
www.garfield.com
Distributed by Universal Press Syndicate
WELL, MARY, I HAVE GOOD NEWS...
© 2002 PAWS, INC. All Rights Reserved.
I'M WEARING BOWLING SHOES!
CLICK
GUTTER BALL

ARE YOU LOOKING AT ME?
NO
I MEAN, YES
www.garfield.com
Distributed by Universal Press Syndicate
I MEAN, MAYBE! I MEAN, IF YOU WANTED ME TO, I WAS! IF YOU DIDN'T, I WASN'T! HELP ME OUT HERE!
© 2002 PAWS, INC. All Rights Reserved.
JIM DAVIS 11-23
I SHOULD'VE ASKED HER OUT
BEFORE SHE STARTED RUNNING

Garfield®
YOU KNOW, SOME FOLKS WOULDN'T SEE THIS FOR WHAT IT IS
SOME FOLKS WOULDN'T UNDERSTAND THE ASTONISHING RESERVES OF SELF-DISCIPLINE THIS REQUIRES
SOME FOLKS WOULDN'T COMPREHEND THE INTENSE CONCENTRATION INVOLVED
SOME FOLKS WOULDN'T APPRECIATE THE CONDITIONING THAT GOES INTO PRODUCING MUSCLE MEMORY THIS ADVANCED
ARE YOU GOING TO LIE THERE ALL DAY?!
YEEEES. IT'S THE OLD "FEAR-OF-WHAT-YOU-DON'T-UNDERSTAND" SYNDROME
JPM DAVPS 11-24
Distributed by Universal Press Syndicate
www.garfield.com
© 2002 PAWS, INC. All Rights Reserved.

I AM NOT LAZY
NOW, WOULD MY CONJECTURE BE MORE CREDIBLE IF I WERE STANDING?
PERHAPS, BUT WE MAY NEVER KNOW
JIM DAVIS 11-25
www.garfield.com
Distributed by Universal Press Syndicate
© 2002 PAWS, INC. All Rights Reserved.

EVER WONDER ABOUT LIFE, GARFIELD?
WHERE WE COME FROM...
WHERE WE'RE GOING...
WHY IT TAKES TWO HOURS TO DELIVER A PIZZA
JIM DAVIS 11-26
www.garfield.com
Distributed by Universal Press Syndicate
© 2002 PAWS, INC. All Rights Reserved.

SIGH...I HAVE NO FRIENDS
HEY, PAL!
ZIP
WISHFUL THINKING
JIM DAVIS 11-27
www.garfield.com
Distributed by Universal Press Syndicate
© 2002 PAWS, INC. All Rights Reserved.

ONCE UPON A TIME, THERE WAS A CAT WHO LOVED TO EAT
HE ATE AND ATE AND ATE
THEN HE EXPLODED
IS THIS MEDICALLY ACCURATE?
JIM DAVIS 11-28
© 2002 PAWS, INC. All Rights Reserved.
Distributed by Universal Press Syndicate www.garfield.com

JIM DAVIS 11-29
COULDN'T FIND A BOOKMARK
I FIGURED THAT
Distributed by Universal Press Syndicate www.garfield.com
© 2002 PAWS, INC. All Rights Reserved.

CHRISTMAS IS COMING SOON
ALL TOGETHER NOW... 1...2...3...
JIM DAVIS 11-30
Distributed by Universal Press Syndicate www.garfield.com
© 2002 PAWS, INC. All Rights Reserved.

Garfield®
HOW ABOUT GOING OUT WITH ME TONIGHT, ELLEN?
WELL, I THOUGHT WE'D TAKE THE BUS DOWN TO THE MALL...
HAVE A ROMANTIC DINNER FOR TWO IN THE FOOD COURT...
–AND THEN VISIT SANTA!
YOU KNOW, ELLEN, SANTA HEARD THAT TOO
AND I BET HE'S BLUSHING
JIM DAVIS 12-1
Distributed by Universal Press Syndicate
www.garfield.com
© 2002 PAWS, INC. All Rights Reserved.

WHAT DO YOU CALL THAT LOOK?
EAGER ANTICIPATION
I DON'T KNOW IF I CAN **TAKE** THAT FOR THE NEXT 23 DAYS
JIM DAVIS 12-2
www.garfield.com
Distributed by Universal Press Syndicate
© 2002 PAWS, INC. All Rights Reserved.

JIM DAVIS 12-3
OKAY, LET'S GO GET A TREE
YOU READ MY MIND!
www.garfield.com
Distributed by Universal Press Syndicate
© 2002 PAWS, INC. All Rights Reserved.

HEY, STRANGER! LONG TIME NO SEE!
JIM DAVIS 12-4
YOU'RE LOOKING GREAT! CAN I GET YOU ANYTHING?
SOME WATER, MAYBE?
www.garfield.com
Distributed by Universal Press Syndicate
© 2002 PAWS, INC. All Rights Reserved.

IT'S NOT THE SIZE OF A PRESENT THAT COUNTS, GARFIELD...
www.garfield.com Distributed by Universal Press Syndicate
IT'S THE THOUGHT THAT COUNTS
© 2002 PAWS, INC. All Rights Reserved.
THINK HUGE
JIM DAVIS 12-5

NOW, BACK TO "ZORGO..."
www.garfield.com Distributed by Universal Press Syndicate
"THE GIANT RADIOACTIVE MUTANT REPTILE WHO SAVED CHRISTMAS"
PREDICTABLE
© 2002 PAWS, INC. All Rights Reserved.
JIM DAVIS 12-6
RAAHHHR!
YOU GLOW BRIGHT ENOUGH, YOU GET TO GUIDE THE SLEIGH

BOYS! HOT CHOCOLATE!
JIM DAVIS 12-7
www.garfield.com Distributed by Universal Press Syndicate
ZIP ZIP
© 2002 PAWS, INC. All Rights Reserved.
WHERE'S ODIE?
I'M STANDING ON HIM

Garfield®
Distributed by Universal Press Syndicate
© 2002 PAWS, INC. All Rights Reserved.
www.garfield.com
GARFIELD, I GAVE YOU THAT GIFT WRAP TUBE TO PLAY WITH!
AND YOUR POINT?
JIM DAVIS 12-8

EGGNOG?
WHY, THANK YOU!
www.garfield.com
Distributed by Universal Press Syndicate
© 2002 PAWS, INC. All Rights Reserved.
JIM DAVIS 12-9

COMING UP NEXT:
"HAIRY LARRY, THE SPIDER WHO SAVED CHRISTMAS"
♪
www.garfield.com
Distributed by Universal Press Syndicate
© 2002 PAWS, INC. All Rights Reserved.
JIM DAVIS 12-10

YOU HAVE REACHED*SANTA'S·WORKSHOP*IF YOU'VE BEEN NAUGHTY, PRESS 1. IF YOU'VE BEEN NICE, PRESS 2
BOOP
YEAH, RIIIIIIIIIIGHT
www.garfield.com
Distributed by Universal Press Syndicate
© 2002 PAWS, INC. All Rights Reserved.
JIM DAVIS 12-11

Dear Santa,
This is Garfield.
www.garfield.com
Distributed by Universal Press Syndicate
Gimme, gimme, gimme, gimme, gimme, gimme, gimme, gimme, gimme.
JIM DAVIS 12-12
HOW'S THAT?
ONE MORE "GIMME" OUGHTA DO IT
© 2002 PAWS, INC. All Rights Reserved.

DOING ANYTHING SPECIAL FOR CHRISTMAS, GRANDMA?
© 2002 PAWS, INC. All Rights Reserved.
www.garfield.com
Distributed by Universal Press Syndicate
NO?... I SEE
JIM DAVIS 12-13
JUST HANGING WITH YOUR PEEPS AND CATCHING SOME BIG AIR DOWN AT THE SKATEBOARD PARK, HUH?
SAME OL', SAME OL'

HO! HO! HO!
www.garfield.com
Distributed by Universal Press Syndicate
© 2002 PAWS, INC. All Rights Reserved.
ELVES
JIM DAVIS 12-14

GARFIELD®
SAY, CAT, COULD YOU PICK UP MY MAIL AND WATCH THE PLACE FOR ME?
—I'M GOING AWAY FOR THE HOLIDAYS
SURE THING. WHERE ARE YOU HEADED?
Distributed by Universal Press Syndicate
I RENTED A LITTLE HOLE AT THE SOUTH END OF THE LIVING ROOM, NEXT TO THE HEAT REGISTER
SOUNDS COZY
www.garfield.com
JIM DAVIS 12·15
WELL, I'D BETTER RUN OR I'LL MISS MY TRAIN... THANKS!
HAPPY HOLIDA—
...TRAIN?
GARFIELD!!
© 2002 PAWS, INC. All Rights Reserved.

YOU THINK?
IT COULDN'T HURT
JIM DAVIS 12-16
www.garfield.com
Distributed by Universal Press Syndicate
...AND A GIRLFRIEND, AND SOME CHEST HAIR, AND A PERSONALITY, AND...
NEVER SAW THE FAT GUY FIGHT BACK TEARS BEFORE
Visit Santa
© 2002 PAWS, INC. All Rights Reserved.

YOU!...YOU, YOU, YOU!!
JIM DAVIS 12-17
www.garfield.com
Distributed by Universal Press Syndicate
IT'S ALL ABOUT **YOU**, ISN'T IT?!
WHAT ABOUT **MY** NEEDS?!!
I THINK I'LL TRY ANOTHER MALL
Visit Santa
© 2002 PAWS, INC. All Rights Reserved.

THEY'RE IN THE OVEN NOW...
JIM DAVIS 12-18
www.garfield.com
Distributed by Universal Press Syndicate
SHOULD ONLY BE ABOUT TEN MINUTES
TEN MINUTES?!
DO YOU REALIZE HOW LONG THAT IS IN "CHRISTMAS COOKIE" MINUTES?!
© 2002 PAWS, INC. All Rights Reserved.

Distributed by Universal Press Syndicate www.garfield.com
JIM DAVIS 12-19
♪WEEEEE WISH YOU A MERRY CHRISTMAS, WE WISH YOU A MERRY CHRISTMAS...♪
© 2002 PAWS, INC. All Rights Reserved.

© 2002 PAWS, INC. All Rights Reserved. JIM DAVIS 12-20
WHO GOES THERE?
EEEK!
www.garfield.com Distributed by Universal Press Syndicate
GARFIELD! I WAS JUST GETTING A GLASS OF WATER!
STEP AWAY FROM MY PRESENT, SIR

WHA?
Distributed by Universal Press Syndicate www.garfield.com
THIS IS A DREAM, AND I'M A SUGARPLUM
© 2002 PAWS, INC. All Rights Reserved.
WANNA DANCE?
JIM DAVIS 12-21

Garfield®
www.garfield.com
Distributed by Universal Press Syndicate
GARFIELD
© 2002 PAWS, INC. All Rights Reserved.
JIM DAVIS 12-22
THREE MORE DAYS, GARFIELD
JUST RESERVING MY PLACE IN LINE
GARFIELD

THE TREE IS UP, THE LIGHTS ARE ON, AND NOW IT'S SNOWING!
www.garfield.com
Distributed by Universal Press Syndicate
THERE'S ONLY ONE THING MISSING...
© 2002 PAWS, INC. All Rights Reserved.
JIM DAVIS 12-23
BRING IT ON, FAT MAN!

CHRISTMAS IS ALL ABOUT TRADITION...
Distributed by Universal Press Syndicate
www.garfield.com
DING-DONG
JIM DAVIS 12-24
-AND THAT WOULD BE OUR TRADITIONAL CHRISTMAS EVE BARBEQUE PEPPERONI WITH DOUBLE CHEESE
© 2002 PAWS, INC. All Rights Reserved.

IT'S CHRISTMAS!
www.garfield.com
Distributed by Universal Press Syndicate
JIM DAVIS 12-25
JOIN ME, WON'T YOU?
© 2002 PAWS, INC. All Rights Reserved.

CHRISTMAS TAKES FOREVER TO ARRIVE...
AND THEN IT'S HERE!
AND THEN IT'S GONE!
ANOTHER WEIRD "CAT" MOOD SWING
www.garfield.com
Distributed by Universal Press Syndicate
© 2002 PAWS, INC. All Rights Reserved.
JIM DAVIS 12-26

GARFIELD, DID YOU SAVE ALL THE BOWS LIKE I ASKED YOU TO?
www.garfield.com
Distributed by Universal Press Syndicate
© 2002 PAWS, INC. All Rights Reserved.
JIM DAVIS 12-27

OKAY, SO MAYBE MOM IS GETTING A LITTLE FORGETFUL
IT'S THE THOUGHT THAT COUNTS, RIGHT?...
...RIGHT?
COME CLOSER AND ASK THAT AGAIN
JIM DAVIS 12-28
www.garfield.com
Distributed by Universal Press Syndicate
© 2002 PAWS, INC. All Rights Reserved.

GARFIELD
ELLEN, I NEED A DATE FOR NEW YEAR'S EVE
YOU'VE ALREADY GOT A DATE? WELL, CAN YOU FIX ME UP WITH SOMEONE?
NO, I'M NOT PICKY
RED FLAG
YES, I SUPPOSE I COULD RENT A PLAID TUXEDO...
BIG RED FLAG
YES, I CAN DO ALL KINDS OF ANIMAL IMPRESSIONS...
HUMONGOUS RED FLAG
NO, I DON'T MIND HER MIME TROUPE CHAPERONING US...
AIN'T A FLAG BIG ENOUGH OR RED ENOUGH
JPM DAVIS 12-29
Distributed by Universal Press Syndicate
© 2002 PAWS, INC. All Rights Reserved.
www.garfield.com

HEY, DON'T BE SAD... EVERYONE FEELS THE SAME WAY
Distributed by Universal Press Syndicate www.garfield.com
BESIDES, THEY'LL BE BACK NEXT YEAR
SNIFF
© 2002 PAWS, INC. All Rights Reserved.
I MISS CHRISTMAS COOKIES
JIM DAVIS 12-30

NOT UNTIL MIDNIGHT
Distributed by Universal Press Syndicate www.garfield.com
YOU GOTTA PROMISE ME
© 2002 PAWS, INC. All Rights Reserved.
C'MON, **PROMISE!**
OH, OKAY
JIM DAVIS 12-31

Distributed by Universal Press Syndicate www.garfield.com
© 2003 PAWS, INC. All Rights Reserved.
HAPPY NEW YEAR
NOT FROM WHERE **I'M** STANDING
JIM DAVIS 1-1

I HAVE NO REGRETS, GARFIELD
JIM DAVIS 1-2
DO YOU HAVE ANY REGRETS?
A FEW...
BEGINNING WITH THIS STUPID CONVERSATION
Distributed by Universal Press Syndicate www.garfield.com
© 2003 PAWS, INC. All Rights Reserved.

JUST IMAGINE THE AMAZING THINGS THAT WILL HAPPEN IN THE FUTURE
JIM DAVIS 1-3
LIKE WILL I GET THE SESAME SEED FROM BETWEEN MY TEETH?
Distributed by Universal Press Syndicate www.garfield.com
© 2003 PAWS, INC. All Rights Reserved.

LET'S CELEBRATE!
JIM DAVIS 1-4
YOU'RE FAT
NOT THE EXCUSE I WOULD HAVE PICKED, BUT IT'LL DO
Distributed by Universal Press Syndicate www.garfield.com
© 2003 PAWS, INC. All Rights Reserved.

Garfield
HERE IT IS, GARFIELD!
© 2003 PAWS, INC. All Rights Reserved.
OUR NEW MEGA-HOME ENTERTAINMENT THEATRE
Distributed by Universal Press Syndicate
WE HAVE DIGITAL HIGH DEFINITION, WIDE-SCREEN, CD, VHS, DVD, CD-ROM, SURROUND SOUND...
...AND THEN THERE'S THE BEST PART...
www.garfield.com
JIM DAVIS 1-5
FIVE, COUNT 'EM, FIVE REMOTES!
WE CAN SHARE!

IN THE LONG RUN, I THINK BAD LUCK AND GOOD LUCK EVEN OUT
THUD
JIM DAVIS 1-6
I MISSED THE CHAIR
YOU'RE GOING TO HAVE TO GET ON A REALLY, REALLY, **REALLY** LONG RUN OF GOOD LUCK TO CATCH UP, PAL
Distributed by Universal Press Syndicate www.garfield.com
© 2003 PAWS, INC. All Rights Reserved.

GOING SOMEWHERE?
UH-HUH
AND UNFORTUNATELY FOR YOU, THIS IS IT
JIM DAVIS 1-7
Distributed by Universal Press Syndicate www.garfield.com
© 2003 PAWS, INC. All Rights Reserved.

CRASH!
JIM DAVIS 1-8
WHAT WAS THAT?!
THE NEW PAPERBOY
HE HAS QUITE AN ARM
Distributed by Universal Press Syndicate www.garfield.com
© 2003 PAWS, INC. All Rights Reserved.

JIM DAVIS 1-9
www.garfield.com
Distributed by Universal Press Syndicate
© 2003 PAWS, INC. All Rights Reserved.
IF YOU AVERAGE THEM OUT, THEY'RE NORMAL

WELL, CINDY, I AM A LITERARY KIND OF GUY
JIM DAVIS 1-10
www.garfield.com
Distributed by Universal Press Syndicate
ACTUALLY, I'M WRITING MY MEMOIR
© 2003 PAWS, INC. All Rights Reserved.
I'M UP TO MY THUMB-SUCKING YEARS
THAT'S THREE CHAPTERS

ANY REQUESTS?
JIM DAVIS 1-11
© 2003 PAWS, INC. All Rights Reserved.
www.garfield.com
Distributed by Universal Press Syndicate
YEAH! HOLD STILL!

GARFIELD
JON. JON ARBUCKLE!
DON'T YOU REMEMBER ME?
UH...NO!
IT'S ME... BERTHA!
I'VE LOST 200 POUNDS!
WOW
WELL, GOTTA GO! GOOD TO SEE YOU
YEAH...YOU TOO
WOW...
I CAN'T BELIEVE SHE WOULD LET HERSELF GO LIKE THAT
JPM DAVPS 1-12
Distributed by Universal Press Syndicate
www.garfield.com
© 2003 PAWS, INC. All Rights Reserved.

IS IT MY TURN TO DECIDE WHAT WE DO TODAY?
YES
BUT IT'S MY TURN TO SAY I DON'T WANT TO DO IT
www.garfield.com
Distributed by Universal Press Syndicate
© 2003 PAWS, INC. All Rights Reserved.

THE BEST THINGS IN LIFE ARE FREE!
HOW MUCH WOULD THE **SECOND**-BEST THINGS COST?
www.garfield.com
Distributed by Universal Press Syndicate
© 2003 PAWS, INC. All Rights Reserved.

YOU'RE IN MEDIUM-SIZED TROUBLE, MISTER!
RATS
THAT WAS HARDLY WORTH THE EFFORT
www.garfield.com
Distributed by Universal Press Syndicate
© 2003 PAWS, INC. All Rights Reserved.

IT'S ONE OF THOSE RESTLESS NIGHTS
Distributed by Universal Press Syndicate www.garfield.com
WHEN THE WEIGHT OF THE WORLD COMES DOWN ON YOU
© 2003 PAWS, INC. All Rights Reserved.
LIKE WHAT IF THE REFRIGERATOR EXPLODES?
JIM DAVIS 1-16

YOU'RE GETTING FATTER
Distributed by Universal Press Syndicate www.garfield.com
I AM?
© 2003 PAWS, INC. All Rights Reserved.
JIM DAVIS 1-17
WHEW! I THOUGHT THE WORLD WAS SHRINKING!

I HAVE DISDAIN FOR YOU
JIM DAVIS 1-18
Distributed by Universal Press Syndicate www.garfield.com
© 2003 PAWS, INC. All Rights Reserved.
UNLESS "DISDAIN" MEANS SOMETHING GOOD

Garfield
...SO I TOOK HER TO THIS FANCY RESTAURANT AND EVERYTHING WAS GOING FINE...WHEN I MISSED MY MOUTH AND STUFFED A BREADSTICK UP MY NOSE
MY DATE LAUGHED AND INHALED AN OLIVE. I JUMPED UP TO HELP HER, NOT REALIZING I HAD TUCKED THE TABLECLOTH INTO MY PANTS
WELL, THAT KNOCKED THE CANDLE OVER, SETTING THE TABLECLOTH ON FIRE
SO I GO RUNNING THROUGH THE RESTAURANT TRAILING A BLAZING TABLECLOTH WHEN THE SPRINKLER SYSTEM GOES OFF
NOW, EVERYBODY STARTS SCREAMING AND DIVING OUT WINDOWS, AND MY DATE...WELL...
DO YOU KNOW WHAT A REALLY WET, REALLY MAD SHEEP DOG LOOKS LIKE?
FIRST DATES ARE ALWAYS SO AWKWARD
JPM DAVPS 1-19
Distributed by Universal Press Syndicate
© 2003 PAWS, INC. All Rights Reserved.
www.garfield.com

THIS SANDWICH TASTES FUNNY
www.garfield.com
Distributed by Universal Press Syndicate
YOU THINK YOU HAVE PROBLEMS...
© 2003 PAWS, INC. All Rights Reserved.
JIM DAVIS 1-20
I HAVE PEANUT BUTTER BETWEEN MY TOES

THERE'S NOTHING HAPPENING
www.garfield.com
Distributed by Universal Press Syndicate
I FINALLY GOT THE WILDFIRE IN MY SOCK DRAWER UNDER CONTROL!
© 2003 PAWS, INC. All Rights Reserved.
OUT OF THE ORDINARY, I MEAN
JIM DAVIS 1-21

DON'T BOTHER ME
JIM DAVIS 1-22
www.garfield.com
Distributed by Universal Press Syndicate
I SAID, DON'T BOTHER ME!
© 2003 PAWS, INC. All Rights Reserved.
YOU JUST INSIST ON EXISTING, DON'T YOU?!

CHECK IT OUT, GARFIELD
JIM DAVIS 1-23
Distributed by Universal Press Syndicate
www.garfield.com
A TIE IS THE CROWNING TOUCH TO ANY ENSEMBLE
© 2003 PAWS, INC. All Rights Reserved.
AND IF YOU HAPPEN TO HAVE ONE THAT LIGHTS UP...
YOU'LL BE AN EASIER TARGET

JIM DAVIS 1-24
I AM REALLY STRIKING OUT, GARFIELD
www.garfield.com
Distributed by Universal Press Syndicate
EVEN "GAP-TOOTHED GRETTA," THE DISTANCE SPITTING QUEEN, SHOT ME DOWN
TOO BAD
© 2003 PAWS, INC. All Rights Reserved.
SHE ACTUALLY SOUNDS LIKE A FUN DATE

I'M BACK FROM DAMAGING THE NEIGHBORHOOD!
JIM DAVIS 1-25
© 2003 PAWS, INC. All Rights Reserved.
I JUST GOT OFF THE PHONE
www.garfield.com
Distributed by Universal Press Syndicate
WONDERFUL! SAVES ME FROM HAVING TO FILL YOU IN ON ALL THE DETAILS

Garfield®
I BET NOT EVEN YOU COULD BE THIS RELAXED
Distributed by Universal Press Syndicate
www.garfield.com
JIM DAVIS 1-26
© 2003 PAWS, INC. All Rights Reserved.
OK, I'M HUMBLED
DON'T MESS WITH THE MASTER

YOU ARE THE PET, I AM THE MASTER
THE MOST IMPORTANT THING IN YOUR LIFE IS YOUR MASTER'S VOICE
ARE YOU LISTENING?
SORRY, I WAS THINKING ABOUT CEREAL
JIM DAVIS 1-27
www.garfield.com Distributed by Universal Press Syndicate
© 2003 PAWS, INC. All Rights Reserved.

WHERE'S YOUR SMILE, FRIEND?
I MUST HAVE LEFT IT ON MY OTHER FACE
JIM DAVIS 1-28
Distributed by Universal Press Syndicate www.garfield.com
© 2003 PAWS, INC. All Rights Reserved.

JON, DO WE HAVE A TOOTHPICK?
I HAVE BREAD AND HAM STUCK BETWEEN MY TEETH...
...ON SECOND THOUGHT, DO WE HAVE ANY CHEESE?
JIM DAVIS 1-29
Distributed by Universal Press Syndicate www.garfield.com
© 2003 PAWS, INC. All Rights Reserved.

GREETINGS...I AM AN ALIEN LIFE FORM BENT ON WORLD DOMINATION
JIM DAVIS 1-30
www.garfield.com Distributed by Universal Press Syndicate
WHY ARE YOU IN THE REFRIGERATOR?
© 2003 PAWS, INC. All Rights Reserved.
I USED TO BE THE MEAT LOAF
JON!

THAT'S IT. NO DATE
JIM DAVIS 1-31
www.garfield.com Distributed by Universal Press Syndicate
I TRIED EVERY WOMAN I KNOW
HE DID, TOO
© 2003 PAWS, INC. All Rights Reserved.
AND EVEN SOME I DON'T
BOY, WERE THEY SURPRISED

I'M NOT GOING TO SHARE THIS COOKIE WITH YOU
Distributed by Universal Press Syndicate www.garfield.com
GRAB
© 2003 PAWS, INC. All Rights Reserved.
I COULD'VE TOLD YOU THAT
JIM DAVIS 2-1

Garfield
Arbuckle Family Reunion
Z
JON, GIVE YOUR OL' AUNT TRUDY A KISS!
DOC BOY, A PIG? WERE YOU RAISED IN A BARN?!!
...IS THAT A TRICK QUESTION?
...WHAT'S THAT IN YOUR EYEBROW?
Distributed by Universal Press Syndicate
...HOW DID YOU GET RID OF YOUR BUNION?
...A WEED WHACKER
...UNCLE ROY, HAVE YOU SEEN MY CONTACT LENS?
www.garfield.com
© 2003 PAWS, INC. All Rights Reserved.
...I BROUGHT PHOTOS OF OUR TRIP TO SEE THE WORLD'S BIGGEST HAIRBALL
...DO THESE PANTS MAKE MY HIPS LOOK BIG?
URP...
...IT'S NOT THE PANTS, DEAR
JIM DAVIS 2-2
...THEN THE CHICKEN EXPLODED!
...CORN'LL GIVE'M GAS, ALRIGHT
...ISN'T THIS NICE?
SO FAR, NO BRAWLS, NO CALLS, AND NO FALLS
IT'S KINDA LIKE DINNER THEATER, ISN'T IT?

HOW'S THAT HERBAL TEA?
IT'S NOT COFFEE, THAT'S HOW IT IS!
JIM DAVIS 2-3
Distributed by Universal Press Syndicate www.garfield.com
© 2003 PAWS, INC. All Rights Reserved.

AWWW. ROUGH DAY, JON?
CHEER UP, JON!
WAS I SUPPOSED TO SAY THAT?
AT LEAST YOU CARE
JIM DAVIS 2-4
Distributed by Universal Press Syndicate www.garfield.com
© 2003 PAWS, INC. All Rights Reserved.

RIIING
MAY I SPEAK TO THE HEAD OF THE HOUSEHOLD?
SPEAKING
GIVE ME THAT!
JIM DAVIS 2-5
Distributed by Universal Press Syndicate www.garfield.com
© 2003 PAWS, INC. All Rights Reserved.

YOU CAN BE REPLACED
Distributed by Universal Press Syndicate www.garfield.com
ALL RIGHT!
© 2003 PAWS, INC. All Rights Reserved.
THAT WAS AN INSULT
HOW SOON CAN WE HAVE SOMEONE HERE?
JIM DAVIS 2-6

GARFIELD, I CAN READ YOUR MIND
Distributed by Universal Press Syndicate www.garfield.com
YOU'RE THINKING, "WHY DOESN'T JON FEED ME?" ...RIGHT?
CLOSE
© 2003 PAWS, INC. All Rights Reserved.
ACTUALLY, IT WAS, "WHY DOESN'T DORK BOY FEED ME?"
JIM DAVIS 2-7

IT'S AN AMAZING WORLD WE LIVE IN
Distributed by Universal Press Syndicate www.garfield.com
THEY CAN PUT A MAN ON THE MOON...
© 2003 PAWS, INC. All Rights Reserved.
YET THEY CAN'T MAKE A COMPUTER THAT BOUNCES
WHAT WAS THAT CRASH?
JIM DAVIS 2-8

GARFIELD
JON ARBUCKLE
Man of action...
...MEMBER OF THE INTERNATIONAL HALL OF HUNKHOOD...
Distributed by Universal Press Syndicate
© 2003 PAWS, INC. All Rights Reserved.
...POSTER BOY FOR TESTOSTERONE...
POW!
SPLAT!
OUCH!
BONK!
THUD!
BAM!
...ABLE TO TAME THE WILDEST HEARTS!
YAAAHHH!
www.garfield.com
ANOTHER ONE OF THOSE "HOW-DID-MY-LIFE-WIND-UP-LIKE-THIS" DREAMS?
JIM DAVIS 2-9

I'VE INSTITUTED MY FIRST TIME-SAVING MEASURE, GARFIELD
www.garfield.com
Distributed by Universal Press Syndicate
ARE YOU READY FOR THIS?
...AS I'LL EVER BE
JIM DAVIS 2-10
© 2003 PAWS, INC. All Rights Reserved.
ONE BUTTON!
IT WOULD BE CRUEL TO TELL HIM ABOUT PULLOVERS

SAD, LONELY, OR SICK...
GARFIELD
www.garfield.com
Distributed by Universal Press Syndicate
IF I HAD TO CHOOSE ONE...
GARFIELD
© 2003 PAWS, INC. All Rights Reserved.
I'D PICK LONELY
IS THAT A SHOT?
GARFIELD
JIM DAVIS 2-11

THIS DAY IS GONE, GARFIELD
I THOUGHT IT WOULD NEVER LEAVE
www.garfield.com
Distributed by Universal Press Syndicate
WE CAN'T RELIVE IT
RELIVE "BORING"?
JIM DAVIS 2-12
© 2003 PAWS, INC. All Rights Reserved.
IT'S GONE FOREVER
LOCK THE DOORS IN CASE IT WANTS TO COME BACK

YOU ARE INSOLENT!
www.garfield.com
Distributed by Universal Press Syndicate
WHY THANK YOU!
© 2003 PAWS, INC. All Rights Reserved.
ANOTHER ADJECTIVE TO ADD TO MY RESUMÉ
JIM DAVIS 2-13

PEOPLE SEEK ME OUT FOR FINANCIAL ADVICE
www.garfield.com
Distributed by Universal Press Syndicate
© 2003 PAWS, INC. All Rights Reserved.
DID YOU TAKE MY WALLET?!
I WANT A LAWYER
JIM DAVIS 2-14

JON SAYS WE DON'T HAVE TO GO OUT TO HAVE FUN
www.garfield.com
Distributed by Universal Press Syndicate
JON SAYS EVERYTHING WE NEED IS RIGHT HERE
© 2003 PAWS, INC. All Rights Reserved.
JON SAYS IT'S FUN-WITH-HAIR-GEL DAY
JIM DAVIS 2-15

Garfield
GOOD MORNING. IT'S SUNDAY, AND YOU KNOW WHAT THAT MEANS...
Distributed by Universal Press Syndicate
A HUMONGOUS NEWSPAPER WITH COLOR FUNNIES...
AND...AND...
www.garfield.com
AAAND...
AND THAT'S ALL
© 2003 PAWS, INC. All Rights Reserved.
BUT THAT'S ENOUGH!
JIM DAVIS 2-16

I AM THE GHOST OF HAMBURGERS PAST, HERE TO SHOW YOU THE ERROR OF YOUR WAYS!
www.garfield.com Distributed by Universal Press Syndicate
GULP!
© 2003 PAWS, INC. All Rights Reserved.
NEEDED MORE OF THE GHOST OF KETCHUP PAST
JIM DAVIS 2-17

PAPER, MISTER?
JIM DAVIS 2-18
www.garfield.com Distributed by Universal Press Syndicate
© 2003 PAWS, INC. All Rights Reserved.
I WONDER WHAT THE HEADLINE WAS
"CAT SHREDS NEWSPAPER"

THERE ARE SOME QUESTIONS IN LIFE I GUESS I'LL NEVER KNOW THE ANSWERS TO...
JIM DAVIS 2-19
Distributed by Universal Press Syndicate www.garfield.com
LIKE, "WHAT'S THE CAPITAL OF NORTH DAKOTA?"
© 2003 PAWS, INC. All Rights Reserved.
I CAN NEVER GET THAT ONE
I'M DROWNING IN BOREDOM, AND HE'S HANDING ME ANCHORS

I THINK SETTING GOALS IS VERY IMPORTANT
Distributed by Universal Press Syndicate www.garfield.com
GOOD IDEA
JIM DAVIS 2-20
WITHOUT A GOAL, HOW WOULD YOU KNOW WHEN YOU FAILED?
© 2003 PAWS, INC. All Rights Reserved.

SEE THE BUNNY SLIPPER, GARFIELD?
JIM DAVIS 2-21
Distributed by Universal Press Syndicate www.garfield.com
THE BUNNY IS SAD BECAUSE HE CAN'T FIND HIS FRIEND
© 2003 PAWS, INC. All Rights Reserved.
DO YOU KNOW WHERE HIS FRIEND IS?
IT'S JUST A HUNCH, BUT YOU MIGHT CHECK THE GARBAGE DISPOSAL

GARFIELD, WHERE'S THE CANARY, AND WHAT'S THAT ON THE FLOOR AROUND YOU?
JIM DAVIS 2-22
Distributed by Universal Press Syndicate www.garfield.com
© 2003 PAWS, INC. All Rights Reserved.
I'M SHEDDING FEATHERS! I'M SHEDDING FEATHERS!

# FOR the BIRDS

Save a statue.
Eat a pigeon.

Tastes like
chicken.

How do I get
out of this
chicken outfit?

Breakfast
is served!

Ever have a
canary go down
the wrong pipe?

NAP TIME...